JOHN K GENDA

© 2019

Unless otherwise noted, all Scripture is from the King James Version, Public Domain.

Scripture marked NKJV is taken from the New King James Version®. Copyright © 1982 by Thomas Nelson. Used by permission. All rights reserved.

Scripture marked NIV are from THE HOLY BIBLE, NEW INTERNATIONAL VERSION®, NIV® Copyright © 1973, 1978, 1984, 2011 by Biblica, Inc.® Used by permission. All rights reserved worldwide.

Scripture marked ESV is from The Holy Bible, English Standard Version. ESV® Text Edition: 2016. Copyright © 2001 by Crossway Bibles, a publishing ministry of Good News Publishers.

Editing by Pam Lagomarsino, www.abovethepages.com

Copyright © 2019 John K Genda
Published by John K Genda publishing
Visit http://www.johngenda.org/

ISBN-13: 978-0-9747224-1-2 for publication
ISBN-10: 0-9747224-1-3 for reference only

Dedication

To the only wise God our Saviour,
be glory and majesty, dominion, and power,
both now and forever.
Amen.

My Dear Beloved,

I write to you about dating at the cross to introduce you to the best life dating at the cross of Christ can offer. Despite your past or current shortcomings, the power of the completed cross of Christ is able and available to give you a new or revived beginning. Humanity is naturally associated with flaws and mistakes. When I think about my faults and deficiencies, I thank God for the cross.

Dating at the cross is not a program, formula, or steps for seeking a mate. It is a lifestyle of spontaneous love, romance, and satisfaction found only at the cross as the power of the Holy Spirit denies the person of self access to the relationship. It is one of excitement, passion, and fullness of joy in the resurrected life.

It is my prayer that God will connect you to a date way beyond your expectation with whom you can experience His spontaneous love in the fullness of joy.

John Genda

Table of Contents

♥1♥
THE WORLD HAS DATING WRONG

When it comes to dating, I would confidently say the world has it completely wrong. No amount of natural education, intellect, or wisdom can deal with the sin nature of self in any relationship. For those who may disagree, check this out. When I typed the word dating on Google, I received 4,780,000,000 results in a few seconds. Some topics were matchmakers, relationship coaches, connection bridges, and much more.

I am not saying all knowledge is useless. Information may be useful in one way or another, but no information is elevated above the cross which is the will of God. The experience of others may help, but not as perfect as the experience of the cross. In fact, trying to apply the experience of a million people in your life will leave you confused.

There is a complete difference between the world's concept of dating and that of the cross. The world says, do what you like. Treat yourself, do what makes you happy. Life is short, live your life. In other words, the world is saying try to watch out for yourself. Gain all for yourself. But the cross says "not my will, but Yours."

The world forgets to warn you that a life built on self is short-lived and lost. Adam had a short life of self, and he lost it all. The cross says lose yourself, and you will have a better life. The world's view of dating is completely based on self. It is all about focus on yourself—celebrate yourself, treat yourself, and worship yourself. Worldly dating is about what people want, not what God wants.

The world comes up with steps, formulas, and programs as a requirement for chemistry or compatibility. They say "if you do this or that, the other person will be happy." It is possible for people to reciprocate kindness, but they have no power over another person's sin nature. This explains why people go out of their way in seeking what they want in someone else but still fail.

Highly educated people, successful business folks, and politicians have given away and invested so much in exchange for a relationship of their choice, but failed. Why? Because the oneness of the cross was never achieved. Due to the world's failure to achieve oneness, it has settled for cohabitation and casual relationship setups. They say again, "Let us just live together, let us do what we want to do together, and let us do what each individual likes to do with others." They say as long as you are happy and independent in any setup is what matters. They accept divisiveness ignorantly since they have no cross that provides oneness.

The world's view of dating is based on research. If research could perfectly predict changes in human sin nature, our world would be perfect. If that were the case, there would be no need for law enforcement. The government will know potential problems and prevent them at the thought level. If the world were also correct about human nature as it relates to dating and marriage, the statistics of broken relationships and marriages would be much less. Despite the overflowing market of expert advice on dating and relationships, the statistics of successful marriages have declined. Why? Because the world is sick and can't heal itself. It is common sense to realize that someone suffering from the same disease he is claiming to heal just doesn't have the answer. Self can't heal itself. The only answer for self is the cross.

The world never considers the interaction between one's soul, spirit, and body when it comes to dating. The world cares less whether one's soul, body, and spirit are operating in unity. They care about people obtaining outside things and status they think will make them feel confident and good about themselves, regardless of the confusion and dysfunction within.

Matchmakers or relationship coaches are unable to predict the future, and can't see beyond their limited experiences or knowledge. Without the cross in their lives, these coaches need help themselves. How can some intellectual who is dysfunctional from the inside help others become whole? Who needs to go through a billion materials on dating to make an informed decision about a good or bad relationship?

The world does not have the cross and can't achieve oneness, so they settle for cause and effect of human sin nature. It is very dangerous for Christians to seek and listen to worldly voices that promote living for self. Fenelon once said that "The voice that suggests living for yourself is more powerful than the voice of the serpent."[i]

The world's view of dating is external, pleasurable, sinful, and full of lust. It is dating that starts externally and attempts to make the failed internal journey. There is nothing internal to connect to the other person outside of external things. It is an outside life built on outside images and things. Worldly dating is a lower life of images, things, and feelings. The person of the world is built with images, things, pride, merchandising, feelings, entertainment, and status. This outside life of the natural man of sin blinds one from seeing the real life from within.

We can't see our real life without being born again. As we become regenerated, our eyes become spiritually opened to see the fake life we have naturally grown to become. The purpose of Christian dating is not just external but an internal reality that leads to eternity.

It can be very challenging to know the path of the cross if we are not willing to renounce things God doesn't approve of. To get rid of things God doesn't want in our lives involves dealing with self. A life without continuous communion and interaction with God is easily deceived to fall into the world's seduction.

♥2♥
DATING AT THE CROSS NEVER FAILS

There is no failure in Christian marriages where the cross is taken daily, and Jesus is followed continuously. If Christian marriages fail, it is not because of Jesus or the cross. It is because one or both spouses drops the cross. When people stop following Jesus, they drop the cross, take up self, and open a door for Satan. That is why God should never be blamed for a broken Christian relationship.

The body of Christ was broken at Calvary for the wholeness of a Christian in all aspects of life. Broken relationships within the church or among Christians is solely due to self of individuals and has nothing to do with God. While it is possible for people who start at the cross successfully to fail when they drop the cross, the cross itself never fails when taken and accepted in every situation. There is a reason why Jesus emphasized we take the cross daily if we wish to follow Him. Jesus never told us to take the cross once in a while or at our convenience but to take it daily.

We can't move from the presence of God, stop serving Him, and expect the same communion we had with Him when we served Him. This explains why most Christian relationships fail. This may help those who wish to argue that Christian marriages fail as well. Although Isaac and Rebekah were put together in God's will, they had a rocky marriage later in life when their children were born. From their life's story, we saw several instances where the will of God was not taken daily. If Christians neglect God's counsel for worldly counsels about relationships, they are bound to revive self which will drown their relationships.

There have been failed relationships between people who met at the church. They prayed together and read the Bible together during the dating period. But shortly after marriage, things fell apart. Several questions emerge in such situations. Where did they miss it? Were both individuals committed to the cross in the first place or was it just for show?

Whenever the cross is dropped, and Satan steps in, there are problems: "The thief cometh not, but for to steal, and to kill, and to destroy: I am come that they might have life, and that they might have it more abundantly" (John 10:10). When self is left in a relationship, it steals it, kills it, and destroys it. Satan in the person of self can bring much drama and worldly influences into a relationship for only the purpose of destroying it. For a Christian relationship to never fail, one must offer obedience to the cross. It may not always be easy to obey the cross, but the willful obedience leads us to the joy set before us.

God knows the area of self you have made into a god in your heart and wants to deal with it. Until He knocks out and tears down the idol of self, you are not ready for a healthy relationship. Deny your idol, take the cross to put your idol to death, and follow Christ. Idols destroy relationships.

Let us pray for strength to be willing to count our lives a loss when it matters for Christ and His kingdom. We must allow God to work in us through the cross of His Son in whatever state we happen to find ourselves. We must purpose in our hearts and actions to say no to self and yes to God.

♥3♥
GET OUT OF SELF

Christians who wish to honor God may want to date, but how does one acknowledge God and date in today's culture where self is promoted and celebrated? The battle of the vanity of ego and selfishness vs the reality of the cross is what Christians everywhere face today, and that includes singles. To date according to the cross, one must leave self out of the equation.

Self is the person we have grown to know since birth. We were born in sin and in the person of sin, which is self. We have been growing, developing, and maturing to the person of self. The environment, culture, family, religion, and society we grow up in all contributed to developing the person of self. This growth process is accompanied by the motions of sin that once worked in us by nature.

The person of self and its baggage of problems and issues must not be taken into a dating relationship by anyone. We must shatter and reject this person of self we have built because it is unfit for any healthy relationship.

Dating at the cross begins when one denies the person of self from coming into a dating relationship, takes the cross, and follows Jesus (Luke 9:23). Jesus knows self and its issues better than we do; hence He mandates us to leave the person of self behind if we need His counsel and leading in dating—period.

Leaving self behind opens our eyes to see the immutable and everlasting spontaneous love of God as the foundation and source of pure and true love. The beauty of God's love is highly elevated above the expectation of unstable self-love. Jesus cares and wants you to have full joy you can find only by taking the daily cross. No relationship needs self because self cannot provide the joy experiences at the end of the cross. Love at the cross is not searching for the reflection of one's self-image. It is seeking God's spontaneous love within people. The spontaneous love of God does not emanate from self-love.

Outside the daily cross, we are deeply in love with ourselves. Our extreme self-love desires more of itself by setting unrealistic expectations for others. Those in self-will venture to look for more of themselves. As Fenelon said, "If we look and search for perfection in others, we will only find disappointment. Our love for others should be based on what God has placed in them, not what they can do for us."[ii]

People of the cross do not live for themselves. They offer themselves as living sacrifices (Romans 12:1). Love in dating should flow out of a living sacrifice. The decision to date at the cross is a decision to offer oneself as a living sacrifice acceptable to God. What a joy when two people offering themselves as living sacrifices acceptable unto God meet at the cross of Jesus Christ. We experience joy as the troublemaker self is kicked out. Yes! You must get out of self to experience joy in dating.

Expecting love or a mate based on the person of self is nothing but the person of sin. The person of self that lies deep within expects a self-fulfilling life from others based on a binding object of self. Self desires to bind itself to others through an object of its personality. Self-love anticipates how others should react to its expectation of a blissful, fun, and enjoyable life. Self says it is all about me. It is about what I want and my satisfaction. Self says "what are you bringing to the table that benefits me?"

The world's system in which we were born of the flesh is all about self; it talks about looking out for yourself, what is in it for you, take care of yourself, look out for number one, and asks how it benefits me. As A.B. Simpson said, "Everything that is selfish, is limited by its selfishness and that if you turn your natural eye upon yourself, you cannot see anything else."[iii] Self-love is bondage and dating in self-love is bondage of both the pursuer and the pursuit. At the end of it all, self loses all as it attempts to gain all. The love of self always results in brokenness and separation.

Dating at the cross is the principle of losing oneself to achieve the best life at the cross while dating in self protects self to lose all at the end. Selfish people are always at the losing end. As it is written: For whosoever will save his life shall lose it: but whosoever will lose his life for my sake, the same shall save it" (Luke 9:23).

Dating in the person of self is full of drama, confusion, issues, and problems. Self has numerous issues of destruction. Some are visible while others are invisible. The person of self we have built can be very deceptive and misleading.

A self-willed person restricts and slows the flow of divine life and love. God does not limit His love from flowing through the cross, but the selfish person does so by their choice of embracing self. Self-love is death, and its selfishness is very destructive.

Self has always been the reason for divorce, separations, and confusion in a relationship. There is no bad relationship or human problem that did not originate from self. If we are truthful enough, we can admit all relationship problems we have ever faced resulted from self. Sometimes it is not always the fault of the other person, but self. Self will never accept it's wrong and always points to the other person. Do you look back and see yourself as the problem in failed relationships? We just love ourselves to the point of not seeing the problem of self within us.

The cross is not only good at dealing with the self within others, but it also deals with self within us. For you to date, you must deal with the self within you. Does it make sense to be in self and desiring a man or woman of the cross? Self-love has no place in the heart to love spontaneously. The heart of self-love is already full of self. Self dates whoever is ready to accept the bondage of self.

The cross says not self but Christ, not flesh but the Spirit, not lust but love. The world says me, myself, I, treat yourself, do what makes you happy, do what you want, live the life you want. If self-love in dating that the world promotes is correct, then we would have a world full of loving, joyful couples. But this is not so. The world is wrong about love because it is unable to resolve the problems that self presents.

No natural born person can deal with self without the cross. The millions of materials on dating and love based on self has not helped but brought great misery and destruction to families and communities. The more people focus on loving themselves, the more miserable and restless they become.

Self cannot see outside of itself, so it searches for a date within itself by looking for people who can relate to the self within itself. Self does not extend beyond the unknown of the natural to the supernatural. Self life is a temporary life as it has no eternal and supernatural connection.

Even when people of self get together, there is never satisfaction because self is present. That is why the majority of married people in self are never satisfied. Their marriage was influenced by the agenda, formula, and programs of self. They thought they were compatible in self. They are restless and always searching because they built everything on self from dating to marriage at the altar. Dating was self that progressed to marriage.

Bernard of Clairvaux once said: "There is no end in search of what is conceived to be desirable from man"[iv] There is never satisfaction with the desires of the natural man. The person of self in which we were born always wants more of the same. If the natural person desires a beautiful woman or a handsome man, there will be no contentment in pursuit of the most beautiful woman or most handsome man. As soon as they come across an individual they consider more beautiful or more handsome, then another man or woman appears to assume those physical qualities.

The process continues on and on until God breaks the chains of destruction. Self is specialized in elevating fake status without any internal reality. One can be married to the most beautiful woman on earth, but self can elevate and create an illusion of another woman to appear more beautiful, which is usually the deception of Satan. How many times have we seen successful men with beautiful wives fall in the trap of appearance?

As a Christian, if you are expecting anything outside the cross in a date, you are already on the wrong footing. This is not to say to just pick anyone who professes to be a Christian but lacks the qualities of a royal priesthood. The way of the cross is always best, and God will exceed your tiny expectations. The infinite God can outperform your finite expectations and anticipation for yourself. But the best God has for you can only be seen at the cross.

It is important to understand God wants you to come out of yourself so that He can show you the best. To attract royalty in God, you must first know and experience royalty at the cross. You must be willing to let go of self. Self can't enter the realm where God wants to take you. The person of self is a natural person and will never understand the things of God.

The things of God are foolishness to self. Self is nothing but flesh, and God has always dealt with people based on flesh and spirit. We should destroy the person of self we have built. Preserving and allowing that person of self to accompany us into a relationship is a potential reason for losing the relationship. In other words, if we fail to destroy self, self will destroy our relationship.

"And he said to them all, 'If any man will come after me, let him deny himself, and take up his cross daily, and follow me. For whosoever will save his life shall lose it: but whosoever will lose his life for my sake, the same shall save it'" (Luke 9:23–25).

Getting out of self means living a life of divine nature, and the life of divine nature comes out of sacrifice. A.B. Simpson clearly explained the life of sacrifice as the law of God. Everything God did, he did out of sacrifice.[v] God is about giving out of Himself. He gave out of Himself in creation. He gave His Son out of Himself for our sins because He and His Son are one. Due to this sacrifice, the love of the cross is uninfluenced. It is not controlled by any social influence of self. This means the physical influence or human formula does not determine the love of the cross. It flows from within and directed by God Himself who is love:

> The love of God is uninfluenced. By this we mean there is nothing whatever in the object of his love to call it into exercise, nothing in the creature to attract or prompt it. The love which one creature has for another is because of something in the object; but the love of God is free, spontaneous, and uncaused.[vi]

We will only understand the uninfluenced love of God as we get out of self. We should look at love based on the purpose of God (2 Timothy 1:9). If we look at love based on self, we will miss the love of the cross in others. The love of the cross is never based on anything in us. There is nothing in us that attracted the love of the cross.

God did not choose Israel because they were prettier or more attractive than everyone. They were the fewest of all people when He chose to love them (Deuteronomy 7:7–8). The love of God is never based on man-made rules of self; it is sovereign. The love of the cross is also everlasting and doesn't change like the love of self. It is continuous. Even in judgment, the love of God is perfect. God is love, and His love is everlasting: "The Lord hath appeared of old unto me, saying, Yea, I have loved thee with an everlasting love: therefore with lovingkindness have I drawn thee" (Jeremiah 31:3).

Past hurts, trust issues, control issues, argumentativeness, anger, laziness, idleness, caring issues, sensitivity, pride, arrogance, intimidation, aggressiveness, nonsense, fake romance or intimacy, lust, sin, impatience, and the materialistic nature of self should be denied in preparation for dating. It is very unfair for the other person if we refuse to acknowledge self or try to hide self in a dating relationship. The only way to deal with self is daily self-denial and cross taking.

Let us stop looking at what to expect from the other person in a dating relationship and focus on the self present in us that may derail a godly relationship. Ask God to show you what is in you that may prevent you from having a healthy relationship.

Self is the number one reason why Christian relationships fail. Being a Christian and listening to those who tell you to embrace the love of self in another to be happy may lead you into deep self-love and not recognizing the cross when it comes. Deep self-love has no clue of the law of sacrifice and the joy set before you as you take the path of sacrifice.

Preparation for dating begins with you, not the other person. You are responsible for getting out of self, not the other person. What a joy when two Christians who are not in self meet. The Scripture makes it clear that in His presence, there is a fullness of joy. We need to guard our hearts against the flesh's desire of showing up in self.

We can understand self better by understanding man as a creature of sin nature (See Romans 3:23). When self is in the leadership of our souls, it aspires to control not only what we do but also who we are. Self desires to constantly want more, have more, achieve more, and be above all based on the natural man. The point here is the desire of self-elevation above others, wanting more from others, and expecting a status above all others.

This is just the devil's nature of pride and arrogance. Here is something from my previous book, *The Mandatory Cross Life,*

> People in self think like the devil: I will control you, I will be better than you, I will have more than you, I will achieve more than you, I will be above you, I will have what others have, and I will be what others are. It is the independent state of our soul from the Spirit of God. It is a soul that relies on self-power. Self is restless, anxious, impatience, crazy, and can strike with sin at any moment. Self is cruel and dehumanizing.

The focus of wanting and achievement is completely on oneself"[vii]

Self is the source of iniquity that will not obey God's will without the daily cross. The cross is the place where one denies self. The attribute of self is to have us deprived of full life due to its selfishness. It is hard to understand we are selfish to ourselves without Jesus. The goal of self is to have us in bondage through desire.

The freedom self promotes is not freedom at all. It is the pursuit of selfish desires and the passion that leads to self-destruction. Self is a fighter and will never be denied without a fight. Daily self-denial is the life of a real Christian and a daily spiritual warfare. Self will always fight back.

When we accept Christ, the conflict begins. He tells us to get rid of our stubborn selves and follow Him. He does not want self to come along because He knows self is full of drama and issues. In other words, Jesus is telling us to get rid of the natural problems and issues of self, which is a sin.

Jesus deals with our conflicting issues, contradicting ideas, and the errors of our ways. Even when we resist, He is there knocking at the door reminding us to get rid of self so that He can get in. For some, Jesus has been knocking for years, but they have refused to let self out so that Jesus can come in. Others have disguised self thinking Jesus will accept their ways. Being full of self makes no room for Jesus. We must empty ourselves of self for Jesus to come in and lead us to the fullness of joy.

For Christian dating to work according to God's will, we must deny self and take the cross. The daily cross we are mandated to take continuously is not the cross of Christ. It is the will of God through Christ in every circumstance. It goes against the will of self. The purpose of the daily cross is to deny ourselves for the sake of Christ and God's kingdom. The daily cross is not something one can give themselves. It is given by Christ each day. We must take the daily cross until we die. That is the only way we will experience joy uninfluenced by self—the joy of the resurrected life.

I would be a liar if I told you taking the daily cross is easy. God's will is not our natural will nor our human nature. God has to help will our spirit toward Him through His Spirit so that we can will to do His pleasure. The Spirit of God has to empower our will to do what God wants. Our part is to hunger and thirst for righteousness through continuous communion with God by prayer, praise, worship, fasting, reading the Bible, and living by faith. Although not easy, a beautiful life comes out of defeating the natural life of self, and you will find great joy.

♥4♥
THE JOY SET BEFORE YOU

One beautiful thing about dating at the cross is joy. God not only gave His Son Jesus a cross for the entire world, but He also set the joy of the cross before Him. The cross of Christ was the will of God the Father, and Jesus fulfilled it perfectly for the joy set before Him; for the joy of your salvation, Jesus fulfilled the cross. Upon fulfilling the cross of the Father, Jesus gives us daily crosses that set joy before us.

We get to this joy daily by denying self, taking the cross, and following Jesus. Accepting the daily will of God leads to daily joy. God wants His children to experience the joy He has set before them, and the only path to reaching and experiencing that joy is through the cross. This is the joy that dating at the cross gives.

Our daily cross is not the cross of Jesus but should be accepted in the likeness of the death, burial, and resurrection of Christ. The purpose of taking the daily cross is a resurrected life. Taking the daily cross may not always be easy. However, if we endure and despise all the difficulties, shame, and distractions, then there is joy before us as we look "unto Jesus, the author and finisher of *our* faith, who for the joy set before Him endured the cross, despising the shame, and is set down at the right hand of the throne of God" (Hebrews 12:2). There is always joy at the end of practicing obedience to the daily cross. The process is not easy at times, but the end is always joyful.

Dating at the cross starts in faith—faith to take the will of God given by Jesus Christ on a daily basis. We should look to Jesus as the author of a good relationship and the keeper of the entire life of the relationship from earth to eternity. Don't let the world deceive you that a Christian relationship is boring. It may be boring when there is no cross or when the cross is dropped. The Bible is clear that there is no peace to the wicked and that includes dating in self.

♥5♥
SELF VS SELF DATING STEALS YOUR JOY

Just imagine the drama that unfolds when people in self decide to date each other. Think about the restless, stubborn, and opinionated role self will play in a self vs. self relationship. First, each individual is full of self which opens two doors for Satan to get into a relationship. Each person has their own expectation of the other person. Such expectations hinder the path to joy. Divine expectation leads to joy.

The self and self scenario creates a tug of war due to obstinate self-interests because both individuals refuse to deny themselves, take the cross, and follow Jesus. In a self versus self relationship, Jesus is not provided the opportunity to lead the relationship. Although some people may continue in a tug-of-war dating, the objective is usually an object they desperately desire from the other person, and the relationship will shortly fall apart when the object is fulfilled or unfulfilled. Tug of war dating is warfare, not joy.

The wise or true believer not in self will notice something is wrong with the whole picture and break up things quickly. The daily cross will point the flashlight on you to see what is wrong with you first. If you are not in self and nothing is wrong with you, you will not be putting up with another self in a tug-of-war dating mess as that hinders your joy.

The very stubborn, brainwashed, and deceived will see nothing wrong with themselves or with the self of their date. They follow the lust and infatuation of their deceitful hearts in an attempt to have their way. The way of lust does not lead to the joy of the cross.

If you are a cross-bearing Christian, you should not be talking about having a fight with your date or arguing all the time. If you are already having a fight in dating, why would you want a marriage of fights? To me, it sounds more of a wrestling match than a date. The tug of war or messy relationships Christians tend to emulate from the entertainment industry or media is not of the cross. It is of self and not Christian. Let God reveal the stronghold of self on your life and repent. The journey of dating progresses to joy as self is removed.

The strength and level and influence of self in each person may vary depending on the level of sin practiced and exposed from the same sin nature. Since birth, several factors contribute to the development of self out of our sin nature. Being in yourself and dating someone who is also in self, is what I call tangling with two selfs. Self is what Satan uses to get to us. Satan now has two outlets to get to a self vs. self relationship. As Satan gets into the relationship, he designs self-love based on standards, formulas, and programs. Each person has to subdue to the program or formula of the love of the other person for things to work out. Human standards zap out joy from within because of being built on self.

If things fail and people don't get what they want, they want to blame God when they never wanted what God wanted to begin with. They were in it for self. They preferred temporary happiness than the joy of the cross. Just imagine the pressure of maintaining a relationship by meeting all the standards and requirements of self. The pressure of self has caused many to crash and fall apart due to their passion for what self wants.

As things fall apart and self goes through the pain or difficulties, all they see is themselves. They feel sorry for their pain and how their comfort is disturbed. They never search for what God wants or is doing in times of trouble. Their focus is getting out of trouble.

Even when they come to the altar to cry to God, they come to cry for what they want—not for God to strengthen their will to change themselves. They cry selfishly to God because they did not get what they wanted. Their joy is lost due to self and selfishness. They feel the other person got more out of the disobedient, selfish relationship. They fail to see their disobedience in refusing to take the cross by maintaining the pride that life is all about what they want. The nation of Israel did the same thing. They cried to God only when they wanted help or deliverance from their enemies, not to get out of self. Joy would never be the destination as long as self remains.

The life of self is full of strife, drama, and ongoing stress. Self is stubborn, and that is why we need the daily cross to push back the resistance of self to God's leading. The desires of self are unlimited and nonstop. A.B. Simpson says it very well: "Time would fail to tell of selfish desires, covetousness, selfish motives, selfish possessions, our property our own, our children our own, and they give us loads of trouble, and care and worry because we insist on owning them."[viii] Dating in self insists on having one's way at the expense of the other. It's about insisting on taking ownership of the relationship from the other person. Self dating wants to build the joy of the other person based on self.

More people are in a self versus self dating relationship than we can imagine. Two people in self dating actually involve four or more people. Just imagine how confusing a dating relationship would be if it involves more than two people. Well, dating in self actually involves more than two people. And there is never joy in a relationship influenced by multiple people in self.

The first two people involved are the individual selfs each person has built since birth. The second two people are the selfs they have built out of expectation of each other—that's four people in total. The other people involved are the persons or idols outside the four people built through entertainment, culture, society, lust, and past relationships. With so many people of self, joy is never reached.

In other words, the number of people self can bring into a relationship can be numerous. Some bring the person of their past relationships, the person of their friends, or the numerous persons of worldly cultures and entertainment. Spiritually, many persons of self can be brought into a dating relationship, and if such people are not crucified with Christ, they will lead to disaster. Although we may not physically see all the many persons of self in a relationship, they are real. They show up in our thoughts and imaginations. We must deal with and cast them down. You must detach yourself from self to date correctly at the cross. Satan, through self, can use others to steal the joy of a relationship.

There have been several instances where people want their mates to be and act like the self or image they have built. Some come into a relationship as one person and try to build another person within the relationship. It is very ungodly for Christian women or men to be saying "I like women like this or that or I like men like this or that." This sends a signal they are in self and a state of unrest. This might be an indication of unpreparedness to settle down with a single individual. When people compare you or your desires to others, it means they are not content with you. They have a lust problem. If you go out on a date and your date fixes their eyes on other people, then that is a sign of problems to come. They have not reached the joy of the cross.

Adam and Eve had no uncles, cousins, mothers, and fathers to bring into their relationship, but the entrance of self through Satan drowned their relationship. If one self can drown a marriage, how much more when too many selfs get involved?

You will never know whether your date is in self if you are in self. Self attracts self. In other words, Satan's attributes attract those living by his attributes. "And if Satan cast out Satan, he is divided against himself; how shall then his kingdom stand?" (Matthew 12:26).

Satan is all about, "I will do this, I will be that, and I will go here and there to do what I want." Our world is full of such boastful individuals living for themselves who have no clue whether they will be alive or dead tomorrow. Their idea about dating is all temporary fantasy. Dating is only an external concept to the self-centered. They pattern everything after their vain imaginations according to the external world they see. The external concept of dating is stagnant toward the joy of the cross.

The blindness or mask over their eyes prevents them from seeing the stronghold of self they wish to date. All they see is their desirable external qualities and presentations of themselves. They fail to see the absence of divine connection in their lives. They may talk about knowing Jesus, but their hearts are far from the truth.

The only way to notice self and its destructive nature is to get out of self, take the cross, and follow Jesus. A relationship of the cross involves dealing with ourselves more than the other person. We must offer ourselves to the daily cross Christ gives us. By faith, we must accept the unpleasant transformation of the cross to avoid the deception and destruction by self. Continuous prayer and practicing God's ways with the help of His Holy Spirit within us will help us see not only what is wrong with us, but also the situation. We can only grasp the joy set before us by way of the cross. Be encouraged to look unto Jesus, despise self, and endure the cross He gives you for the joy He sets before you. If you endure, there is joy set before you.

♥6♥
SPONTANEOUS LOVE

The world loves to talk about spontaneous love—a love of which the world is ignorant. Spontaneous love at the cross is not a planned event of self. It is who a person is. It flows naturally like spring water without a tap to restrict its flow. We can only find spontaneous love at the cross.

Spontaneous love is the same at every angle, every moment, every day, in every situation, and at all times. It is the same in both good and bad times. This love is never based on worldly passions, emotions, activities, and affections. The emotions and affections of spontaneous love are pure from within.

Spontaneous love flows from God and God alone who is unlimited in love. God never gets tired of loving and showing us His love. He will never run out of love. God will not say "I just came from work, and I am tired, so My love can't flow to you." God Himself is love (1 John 4:8). God gives us His Spirit to love spontaneously. He lives in His children so that love can flow through them.

Those walking in the path of the cross and following Jesus should have no problem loving spontaneously because God supplies them with unlimited love. It just flows.

The Bible is clear and simple about this. When we get out of ourselves, everything in a relationship flows like pure water. There is no worldly tap to control love at the cross. If you truly want to experience spontaneous love, take the cross. Spontaneous love eradicates arguments and debates because it just flows. It flows from sunrise to sunset and acts of loving kindness are fulfilled without coercion.

Love should flow with dating at the cross at all times. No worldly formula or programs is needed for the flow of pure divine love in the dating period. Love just flows out of a person walking in the path of the cross. The love that flows is life because Jesus is the resurrection and the life.

When true sanctified Christians date each other, the love of life that flows is unexplainable. This pure love from God can satisfy all emotional needs. It is love that knows how to respond to the feelings of the other person without being taught, instructed or lust. Since it flows from God, it sees and identifies where life is needed in the other person, and it flows right there. There is no pulling of teeth or legs just to show loving kindness. It flows on its own. Divine love identifies needs and flows to fill those needs in an unexpected manner.

If you are always telling people how to love you and respond to your emotions and feelings, then you may need to reconsider the dating. The dating of two sanctified people or individuals is pure and accepted by both individuals because things flow in synchronization. Spontaneous love synchronizes two people at the cross. They are synchronized to live a life God wants.

Real Christians should not be taking love lessons from unbelievers who have no clue of spontaneous love that flows from within. They want to teach spontaneous love based on emotions and feelings of the body. They have no clue that without a living spirit within, the body gets tired and the mind changes due to folks being spiritually dead on the inside. To the unbeliever, love is limited to touch and nakedness. This is a much lower level of worldly love. I am not talking about intimacy in marriage which is also spontaneous.

Spontaneous love is love obtained through death, burial, and resurrection with Christ (Galatians 2:20). Ungodly dating experts do not understand pure spontaneous love because they do not understand the sinful nature of man. They base their predictions on human behavior research. Although knowledge may be helpful, much human effort is required to meet or fulfill recommendations made by experts and philosophers to imitate the spontaneous love God provides naturally.

God does not have to make a plan each time He wants you to experience His love. He does not stand in a corner to receive or study some recommended practice because He is love. He reads no books from popular personalities, experts, idols, or philosophers about love so that He can be familiar with steps or formulas of love. God is love. He loves spontaneously.

Early church fathers or saints understood the power of love at the cross. They not only understood love; they also experienced it in their will by the power of the Holy Spirit. True love is more than just agreeing to be together, and it is not a mere commitment of words or going around saying "I am taken." It is an affection of a regenerated soul: a soul that has come alive from a living spirit within. As Bernard explains in his work on the *Love of God*: "Love cannot evolve from a mere contractual agreement together, for it is an affection of the soul. It cannot be gained in this way. Love is spontaneous in origin and impulse, and so it frees us to recognize that true love is its own satisfaction."[ix]

God provides a resting place of holy love for a Christian in the path of the cross. There is no need for a Christian to be restless in pursuing and searching for spontaneous love. Spontaneous love comes from the resurrected life.

Come to Jesus and accept His easy love. If you are tired and burdened with the demands of love the world has placed on you, come to Jesus. If you are tired of jumping from one relationship to another and restless without peace, come to Jesus. Come to Jesus. His love is humble and gentle. You will find quietness for your soul. His yoke is easy to bear, and His burden is light (Matthew 11:28–30). Deny yourself, take the cross, and follow Jesus, and you will find true love.

Following Jesus is the only way to cease laboring in seeking love. Allow the love of the cross to flow through you by getting yourself out of the way. Purpose not only to see spontaneous love through the help of the Spirit but to be a person of spontaneous love.

♥7♥
ROMANCE, CARE, AND LOVINGKINDNESS

Personally, I don't think there is anyone more romantic than God. I am talking about pure romance that flows within a regenerated spirit. I am not talking about design romance sold as entertainment to society. Don't allow the world to intimidate or deceive you that Christians aren't romantic or are boring. That is a big lie from Satan. Read "Songs of Solomon" in the Bible and tell me who on earth can match the romance of God?

Christians in the path of the cross should clearly understand the difference between romance and lust. The world's form of romance is lust, and God's form of romance is satisfaction. Romance cannot be taught or designed by self. Self does not understand divine romance.

Professing Christians have often made the terrible mistake of confusing bodily romance as love. Some fell in the trap of marrying people full of lust; they were unable to fulfill themselves. The lustful person used them for a while, and when they are unable to fulfill their constant thirst and passion for lust, they break up. You have no one to blame if you fall for lust.

Lust is something no one can fulfill or satisfy. What can satisfy Satan? Watch out for uncontrollable sexual desires under the disguise of romance. They are addictive, and you will be unable to control them within your date. They will not only lead you to sin but also lead you deeper into sin due to the many lustful demons you may become united with.

Dating at the cross is never to manage or fulfill the sex drive or addictive behaviors of others. Refer them to the cross. They need help not dating.

The problem with man-made romance is unstable progression and multiplication of burdens. There are always more rules and trends to follow. The world says to be romantic is to try this new thing or that new thing. Since it comes from the entertainment of bodily passions, it becomes addictive, wayward, and restless. Man-made romance is from self, and its progression can lead to very ungodly practices and filthiness.

The desire of self to always want more and more leads romantic designers of self to invent new practices to arouse the feelings of bodily passions. Ungodly romance progresses by inventing new ways of stimulating and arousing feelings of the flesh. This type of romance has led to sex and alcohol and drug addictions. Dangerous pills are swallowed to feel a certain way. The body is pressured outside of nature. Healthy bodies are altered to look romantic even when dying slowly within.

The goal of worldly romance is a continuous and everlasting high of the flesh that eventually leads to slow death or sickness. Romance should lead to life, not death. Common sense tells us the body was not designed to be overstimulated by substances or devices. The everlasting feelings of bodily pleasure is a lie from Satan who wishes to destroy people. It is a lie that sex lasts forever. It is a lie that one cannot live and be happy without sex at dating. Do we really need designed romance to be happy daily, do we need mechanics to stimulate our happiness daily? Doesn't it sound like self-imposed slavery?

This is how dangerous self is, and that is why it should never be taken into a holy dating. This should serve as a warning to Christians in the path of the cross who desire worldly ways. The ways of the world will enslave you. Your joy in Christ would be lost. And dating the ungodly will also enslave you. They will expect you to act like a male or female prostitute and subject you to all nastiness and filthiness. If God has saved you from filthiness, don't go back.

Nasty worldly romance has become a huge business. The nastier and filthier it is, the more it sells. Since ungodliness can never be satisfied, it leads to waywardness and excessive burdens of those involved. The wayward inventions of romance have progressed from people to objects and electronic devices.

Unregenerate Christians would fall in the trap of self romance by watching romantic movies and filthy worldly entertainment and see nothing wrong with it. Watching filthy ungodly entertainments is catching filthy spirits. It is uniting your spirit with what you watch and will fill your soul with much darkness. Ungodly images are imaginations that exalt themselves above the ways and purity of God. They should be cast down. If you watch ungodly images to become romantic, you are not ready for dating at the cross. You are under demonic possession. Cast down those imaginations before they become too high for you to bring down.

Romance is a big worldly business. A Google search of the word romance returned 1,040,000,000 results (0.66 seconds). This includes written materials, films, movies, videos, and much more. Should a sanctified Christian spend time on studying the benefits of self that God has told us to deny?

The romance of God is not eros. The Greek love of eros was a dangerous form of uncontrollable addictive burning sexual desire and can also be demonic possession. Even the Greeks considered it dangerous at the time. The Greeks understood that man-made romance was not only self-destructive but also dangerous.[x] History is a witness of the dangers of accepted uncontrollable Greek sexual desires to family and community.

Today, the dangerous, destructive eros form of love is highly celebrated by the entertainment community as it continues to ravage and destroy people and communities. Our youth will give up their entire lives or future before them in exchange for a pill that will give them the eros experience. Christians should be running away from eros and its entertainment. Eros is not romance; it is a sick state of the soul. A lot of Christians have been deceived by the world's view of romance as love. Should the world really be teaching the church romance?

Divine romance that flows out of the cross is highly elevated above the romance of the world which is only limited to bodily pleasures. Divine romance is better and offers much more than sex.

That is why Christians can joyfully date without being naked because real romance is present within and is manifested in kindness and true holiness. It is full of life and excitement. Yes! And when the time comes for sex in marriage, it will even be more romantic, because romance exists outside of sex. If romance is absent in dating and marriage, even sex in marriage means nothing, but a bodily exercise. At the cross, romance is daily and always.

A godly relationship is not frustrating or boring. Disobedience makes romance and loving kindness a burden. The cross addresses intimacy and social needs in oneness at marriage. Romance is always giving your best at all times. In marriage at the cross, intimacy is daily and always. It is more than a few minutes of sexual activity. It is giving love at its best always:

When God gives, He gives His best. A.B. Simpson clearly conveys God as a giver and that the law of God is a law of sacrifice.[xi] God has always been giving out of Himself. He gave Himself in creation; He gave Himself in His Son Jesus for our redemption. All the beautiful natural attractions we see is a result of God giving of Himself.

Understanding God is love, and everything He does is with love, is the beginning of understanding romance. Romance itself is life. We can't give life in everything we do if we have not allowed the life of God to work in us. Going to church or being a leader in the church is not a requirement for God's life. God's life in us flows as we deny self, take our cross (the will of God), and follow Jesus continuously.

Divine love begins with agape love and is broken down into philia in the dating period. Divine love provides an explainable philia (friendship). Philia is the Greek version of love that would be useful in dating, meaning a loyal friendship.[xii] The Greeks considered philia way above eros. A loyal friendship comes from a heart of regenerated kindness and sacrificial service (Galatians 6:2).

God came in the person of His Son Jesus to demonstrate the law of sacrifice by giving Himself as the best. Demonstrating the law of sacrifice was also evident in the lives of those who feared God. Abraham, Isaac, and Jacob would usually give up themselves to chase after the ways of God. On the contrary, Saul, Jonah, Esau, Ishmael, and others in the flesh would not give up self for God's will. Those who gave up self won at the end, and those who refused to let self go lost it all.

Let us not be deceived by the world that being a Christian is not romantic. Again, that is a lie from the devil who hates holy romance. The Song of Solomon teaches divine romance from dating to marriage. It expresses intensity and passion for one another spontaneously. God is concerned for your physical and spiritual needs as well. It just has to be via the way of the cross. Divine romance is fulfilling and joyful. Let us stop giving ourselves headaches over what is not romance. Practicing to be like God our Father through obedience by the help of His Spirit helps us to become a person of love like God, for God is love. All we need to do is ask God to make us love, and He is, and He will do it.

♥8♥
ANIMAL LOVE AND LUST

We live in a society where animalism is celebrated as entertainment. Animalism in dating is the self-willed life of the senses as it relates to outward materials of the natural man. It is based on nothing internal or spiritual. The soul is completely controlled by the senses through self. Self is put on, the cross is dropped, and the path of Christ is abandoned.

Dating at the cross demands the natural man be crucified with Christ and this crucifixion should be experienced continuously by denying self and taking the daily cross. Bernard emphasized the lawless state professing Christians may find themselves in as they abandon the path of the cross for the life of self: "The state turned away from God becomes folly when it is excessively turn in upon itself. It is so wild that it is ungovernable."[xiii]

The goal of Christian dating is not animal love because the animal life of self-life is prohibited from taking the cross and following Jesus. Christians may find themselves in trouble and much problems if they choose a path outside the cross. God's promises in the cross lead to an elevated life far above the lower life the world's love experts promise. The multiplication of worldly dating expert advice has not made people happier because the natural man does not understand God's ways. To make matters worse, the world would never be able to predict and control the natural nature of sin and self. Despite all the expert advice outside the cross about love and dating, the statistics suggest failure. The animal self could not be controlled, tamed, or predicted.

Unfortunately, many Christians refuse to renounce the way of animalism. They settle for it and later complain like the world that there are no good women or men around as if their job was to look for good men and women. Animalism is a creep that destroys a Christian relationship.

Dating at the cross could not be achieved if the animalism within is not surrendered to be crucified with Christ. Animal dating is built on outside physical attributes defined and standardized by the materials of the world. The world sets the benchmark to meet to be considered as being in love. To the world, one's outward and physical attributes should be accepted by the other party to be considered a perfect couple. The origin of everything animal is self-love.

Whatever attribute is considered in Christian dating should pass through death, burial, and resurrection. Let the animal of self be put through death, burial, and resurrection. Those who desire godly dating should surrender the animal of self to the cross. Christian dating cannot be based on the animal stage of mere senses. Put self on the cross when you come into a dating relationship and let God resurrect what He wants to resurrect.

The spirit of Satan, which runs the world, sets the standards for animal love. The source of animal love is not a regenerated person.

Animal love is the preoccupation to achieve satisfaction from physical sensuality. Satisfaction in human sensuality is never achieved. The natural will has no control over wild human sensuality. At the animal stage, the senses demand more and more of the same. That is why worldly benchmarks of self never work.

Self ran by Satan is never satisfied. Self-love is not spontaneous. It is ever adding demands and rules. Who wants to live under constant rules of bondage? A relationship of the cross does not have to be as demanding as the experts have designed. The experts want you bound by their complicated rules to love like an animal. The cross wants to free you from the rules and programs of animal love.

Jesus has mandated Christians to deny self (the animal life), take the cross, and follow Him. We lost our spiritual sense when Adam sinned and died spiritually. All that was left of Adam was intellect of the soul and senses of the flesh. It is impossible for the senses of the body to be subject to the spirit's control when self is alive and active. As Bernard once said: "Animality is a form of life which is dominated by the senses. It is engrossed in the pleasure afforded by material things that it loves, and thus it feeds its sensuality. Since it is accustomed to think only of bodily senses and to assume that nothing exists except what it has left outside or it has brought back into itself, it finds its happiness is possible only in living with bodily pleasures."[xiv]

Christians dominated by the senses should examine themselves to see whether they are selfless or unable to offer themselves to someone else. Approaching a prospective date because you are drawn to their physical figure with burning passion is not love. It is lust. Both the pursuer burning for physical passion and the one being pursued pose a great risk of hurt and failure.

Christian culture is quite different from the world's culture. The world's idea of dating is the satisfaction of lust. The desire is never-ending. It is funny to hear the world say "he does not satisfy me" or "she does not satisfy me." A Christian should ask God for help if they ever find themselves in the satisfaction worldly trap. Fenelon made a very important point that the best way of loving people is to love the God in them. If your love for others is only based on what you expect of them or can get from them, then you are not loving.[xv]

This makes clear sense. If love is based on natural human performance and expectation, then love is of self. The problems that erupt when performance and calculative love fails can be overwhelming. The natural human will fail and disappoint.

Love should never be a reflection of the self-image we have built. The love we experience when Christ abides in us is based on the attributes of God which are usually experienced in humanity as the fruits of the Spirit. God's love is perfect and never based on one's perfection.

♥9♥
SEXUAL ISSUES

Sex is a beautiful thing within the context of a godly marriage. Treating sex casually as a sport and entertainment like the world does can become a bondage. The health of family and society depends on the godly value placed on sex. Let us not let the world fool us that sex is sex and is the same everywhere.

The spontaneous sexual relationship between a holy married man and woman is not the same as a lustful animal relationship in the world. Sex outside of God's plan is the reason for worldly trouble. There is never satisfaction in the animal sexual relationship of the world because it is full of lust and influenced by many spirits of self and its attributes.

A holy sexual relationship in a holy marriage is in one spirit and influenced by only one spirit. No other spirits from the world are brought into it. That is why new Christians with a promiscuous sexual past rushing into a dating relationship to marry for sex can be a problem. First, they have not been delivered from the many spirits they united with while messing around in the world. This is something that should not be ignored. One can be handsome or pretty but with much baggage.

Sexual issues are a serious problem that churches usually shy away from. It is usually not discussed in Bible study because those involved would be offended. It is true that those who desire sexual pleasure for the purpose of marriage may have some serious problems deep within that needs to be dealt with by the precious blood of Jesus. Sexual purity or impurity is also a big issue to be tangled with as a single Christian.

There are several circular materials advising on the issue of sex and sexuality. Although several materials are out there, the choice is usually what we want or what God wants. God has clearly stated in His Word what He expects of Christians about sex. It is very simple. Although simple, it can be very difficult for those who wish to add their own thoughts to make God fit in the box they have designed.

A Christian who loves God or desires to improve a relationship with God should always seek to be what God wants—not what society is telling them to do regarding sex and sexuality. Men and women who serve the Lord should strive to be sexually pure. The purpose of Christian singleness is not to sneak around engaging in sexual pleasures. Sexual issues can affect stability and our walk with God. It can also affect any future relationship.

In 1 Corinthians 7, Paul talks briefly about sex as it relates to singleness. Paul was aware of the problems the church was having with sexual issues and approached the topic with revelation and wisdom. In verse 2, he said, "To avoid fornication, let every man have his own wife, and let every woman have her own husband" (1 Corinthians 7:2). Some people marry for the only reason of not being able to control themselves. It can be hard to say no to situations that one places themselves in. But let us look at what Paul said a few verses later, "I say therefore to the unmarried and widows, it is good for them if they abide even as I. But if they cannot contain, let them marry: for it is better to marry than to burn" (1 Corinthians 7:8–9).

The Christians at Corinth were saved but were also struggling with sexual sins. Paul dealt with the issue in relation to spiritual strength, level, and maturity. First, for those Christians who were unable to control themselves, it was better for them to marry and avoid living in sin. Second, for those who are spiritually mature and have control over their own will and are able to wait without sinning, it is better to wait for God's time. Third, it is not a problem to marry, but if one married just to avoid fornication, they would still have sexual issues with the flesh:

But and if thou marry, thou hast not sinned; and if a virgin marry, she hath not sinned. Nevertheless such shall have trouble in the flesh: but I spare you (1 Corinthians 7:28).

But if any man think that he behaveth himself uncomely toward his virgin, if she pass the flower of her age, and need so require, let him do what he will, he sinneth not: let them marry. Nevertheless he that standeth stedfast in his heart, having no necessity, but hath power over his own will, and hath so decreed in his heart that he will keep his virgin, doeth well (1 Corinthians 7:36–37).

The Corinthian church was full of sexual immorality among church members. They went right on to praise God in their sinful, immoral state, as in many churches today. They were open and proud of their sins. Today is no different. More nasty things exist within churches.

The apostle Paul had to confront the church: He confronted a brother who was having sex with his father's wife within the church.

It is not judgmental to address known and open sin within the church respectfully, especially when there is clear evidence. This is not saying we should police sin or harass others.

People are on a different frame of mind or heart with their sexual needs issues or struggles. Those who struggle with any form of sexual issues not approved by God should seek divine help prior to venturing into a dating relationship. Just because someone comes along claiming they love Jesus, it doesn't mean they are free from sexual filth and issues. Loving Jesus is a practical experience of the daily cross.

This is something singles who love God should be able to discern. Some issues are clear and visible and do not need much discernment. Some hide issues of pornography and lust and carry them into relationships. Some men and women who came from the world to the church have not been completely delivered, and some want to bring their issues in a holy dating relationship. If such a man or woman has not emptied themselves of the self in the world, they may not be ready for stable dating or even marriage. Men who love pornography or women with certain shapes or seductive clothing may need deliverance. Women who love male prostitutes may also need to be delivered. They need to come to the cross for help.

Being sick with sexual lust can cause anxiousness and tons of problems in a relationship. When it comes to sexual purity, both the person struggling and the one who desires to marry them must strive for freedom from sexual bondage.

♥10♥
WHAT IS CHRISTIAN DATING?

Christian dating is when two people are synchronized at the cross as one in God's will and practicing the divine life of following Jesus. By being synchronized as one, I am not talking about a marriage union in the oneness of dating. I am talking about the will of God at the cross.

In Christian dating, each person denies self, takes the cross, and follows Jesus. Then both individuals are spiritually synchronized at the cross as one in God's will. When people take the daily cross, they are taking the will of God given by Jesus Christ, and the will of God is the same in every circumstance. It is about doing what God wants. Christ is the will of God yesterday, today, and forever. It is this will of God that a real Christian dating converges to meet. Christ leads as self is left out.

The people involved in Christian dating are those in whom Christ works His salvation as they work out their salvation on a daily basis. It is critical for those who wish to date to pray for a person already deep in the path of following Christ. Christ leads when both individuals are deep in the path of following Him. They experience deep spontaneous love influenced by nothing. It is this deep spontaneous love that takes dating to marriage and keeps dating in marriage unto eternity because God doesn't change. The will of God in dating flows to marriage and was established at eternity.

Christian dating is not seeking an unbeliever you desire and try to save them so that you can date and marry them. Of all the people dying and going to hell daily, the only soul you care about to save from hell is the one you want to date? Does this not reflect an even deeper love of self? Do you have the power to save? Are you the God of salvation? Why give yourself an unnecessary headache in trying to save someone unto yourself? Through God's sovereign and permissive will, things may come out the way we may expect or do not expect. But according to Scriptures, dating unbelievers is not the perfect will of God (Deuteronomy 7:3, Proverbs 22:25).

God will not force you to choose His perfect will. He wants you to choose His cross out of love for Him. Unfortunately, many Christians have given themselves much pain and sorrow in their mission on saving for dating. In a few cases, people have led their prospective mates to Christ, and it worked for them, but why risk obtaining God's perfect will purposefully? Those for whom saving for dating might seem to work may acknowledge the headache as not God's best. Some are lucky to come across those who truly desire God; I have no formula about people's choices. My advice is don't purposefully take the risk of dating outside of the cross if you are already in the path of the cross.

If you take the risk and things do not work out, be willing to bear the consequences in humility. If it was your fault things didn't work out because you were in self, accept and learn quickly. If things didn't work out because the other person is in self, accept, learn, and grow. The problem also is self is not willing to learn from its own mistakes.

There are also many cases where people pretended to be saved but were never saved. They confessed Jesus in pretension but never believed in their hearts. Such deceptiveness for dating or marrying can be very destructive and painful. The deceptive person will go to church with you, read the Bible with you, or even creep in church leadership—but in self and destructive in every direction.

Some have deep dark lives that can be very overwhelming when discovered or revealed. Therefore, dating should be no rush or desperation. Do not ignore baby signs of self. Baby problems of self are indicators that adult problems do exist. Babies learn from adults.

Christian dating is not coming with a list of pleasures to accomplish before marriage. If you need a list of pleasures to enjoy to be fulfilled as a single before marriage, then you may need to evaluate your thought process and values.

Christian dating is also not a period for trial and testing marriage. It is not a period for moving in together and living like a married couple. The world has made dating as a period of trial and testing of the body. First, how wrong is this picture? A man asks a lady out on a date and already considering a future outing with another woman if things don't work out. He has no interest in committing himself to one person until he's "sowed his wild oats." He believes as a man he's been gifted the freedom to freelance date. Already committing adultery in his heart and mind, thinking about what he wants, and how he can get it. Modern women are also in the same bag of sexual issue, not just men. They want to see dating as the world's prescription of trial and testing. This is an issue.

The problem with dating as a period of trial and testing of self is that the natural person is composed of good and evil. It is possible for good to show up during the trial and testing period for a season until evil shows up. People can suppress self to get what they want, and after that, they care less. It is possible for an individual in the person of self with habits of promiscuity, profanity, and wild parties to conceal such bad habits.

Not every professing Christian within the church is in the path of following Christ. Many have not taken the cross or do not practice self-denial on a daily basis. They depend on the power of self to do what they want and are not submitted to the ways of God. They fail to understand that developing a Christ-like nature is not based on self or human power. Human power is not resurrection power. The will of God is the meeting place for Christian dating.

Christian dating is God-centered and focused on what is right in God's sight by following biblical values and morals. Christian dating is sacrificial in every aspect. It involves self-denial, cross taking, and following Jesus. The concept of the cross-life itself is seeking unity with Christ and with God.

A Christian dating relationship involves giving up of self. The love of the cross is coming out of self to be a burden bearer. "Bear ye one another's burdens, and so fulfill the law of Christ" (Galatians 6:2). We must ask God to help us accept being crucified, dead, and buried with Christ. This is how we will enjoy the full blessings of the elevated life. If God has elevated us in Christ, why should we desire a lower animal programmed life?

Christian dating is never boring when we submit to the cross. It leads to unexplainable satisfaction and joy. Kingdom life not only leads to righteousness but also comes with peace and joy.

♥11♥
TOXIC DATING IS A RED FLAG FOR ABUSE AND DIVORCE

We are not promoting perfection when we talk about toxic dating and red flags; we are talking about common issues known to cause problems in a relationship for generations. These issues are not only known within the church but are known by the world as well. They have existed since ancient times and have not changed as there is no new thing under the sun.

Although Christians live in the kingdom of God, they also live in the world and experience similar problems as the world. Worldly professionals may be aware of relationship problems, but the cross offers the best solution. Let us take a look at some disagreements and toxic issues that may lead to a dysfunctional dating experience and marriage.

A Common Faith

Being forced to debate or give up your faith and values as a requirement to date and marry someone are signs of potential problems in both dating and marriage. People have strong ties to their belief system and values and settling for non-Christian values may turn your heart away from the true and living God. Christians should not be dating anyone who is in opposition to their faith in Jesus Christ or the biblical family culture. This will definitely create conflict in dating, marriage, family, and raising children.

Several professing Christians have married folks who clearly denounce Christ with the expectation of saving their souls, but failed. Agreement or disagreement on faith is a very big thing. The solution to this is simple: do not date someone with a different faith or belief system. You have the right to do so based on your free will, but you are responsible for the risk you take. There are numerous Scriptures that advise against marrying unbelievers or those who do not believe in Jesus Christ: "Do not be yoked together with unbelievers. For what do righteousness and wickedness have in common? Or what fellowship can light have with darkness? What harmony is there between Christ and Belial? Or what does a believer have in common with an unbeliever? (2 Corinthians 6:14–15 NIV). This is plain and simple and further confirmed with, "Do not *intermarry* with them. Do not give your daughters to their sons or take their daughters for your sons" (Deuteronomy 7:3 NIV).

Disagreements within Christian sects and Christian service can spell trouble ahead. Agreement in doctrine and service is very important. There are major lifestyle doctrinal differences within Christian denominations and service. Although the body of Christ is supposed to be one, man's misunderstanding and interpretation of Scriptures have let in too many divisions. Doctrinal differences are something that should not be compromised and should be resolved and agreed upon for dating to proceed. Otherwise, I advise it to be broken.

The pain within in trying to accept what you don't believe in is serious. Some have been in relationships in which one person moved from a false doctrine Christian sect to accept the true gospel, and it worked. Some have followed their heads to doctrines they disagreed with and then found trouble within.

Faithfulness to the service of the cross is very important. How your date participates and supports the body of Christ should be noted. This should be a sign to help you decide. Several professing Christians have made the mistake of marrying someone who just professes to be a Christian but has no passion for participating in the body of Christ. Marrying someone who says they are a Christian but does not pay tithes and does no service within the body of Christ is a mistake. This is a reason why most people go to church alone because their spouses are not interested, and the rebellion flows in the family as it affects the children. God wants the entire family involved in communion with His through the saints.

Your date must respect and value the fellowship of believers. Any mate who reduces your passion for God is not from God. Dating the once-in-awhile churchgoer is not wise. If someone is not faithful to God, they will not be faithful to you in the long run. Oneness in faithfulness to God's will and service contributes greatly to a healthy relationship. How can someone claim to be a Christian or love God when they never consider or discuss the Word of God together during the entire dating period? It is a red flag if couples ignore regular discussions of the Word.

We Need to Talk

Relationship coaches and dating experts often cite communication issues as an ingredient for a toxic relationship. People of the cross should have no problem with communication issues. Paying relationship coaches who are not Christians only to tell you how to talk about communication issues makes no sense. Problems with communication only exist when somebody in the relationship drops the cross.

People should be able to address and discuss small issues before they become monsters. Talking down, name callings, teasing, provoking, disrespectful words, and profane words are not healthy. Someone truly in love with you will not say negative things about you to yourself, friends, and family. There are numerous examples in the Bible of how godly and loving communication should be conducted. Here are a few:

- "Having your conversation honest among the Gentiles" (1 Peter 2:12).
- "Keep thy tongue from evil, and thy lips from speaking guile" (Psalm 34:13).
- "A word fitly spoken is like apples of gold in pictures of silver" (Proverbs 25:11).

Make the other person feel better through simple communication or appreciation. Give love and don't buy love. If you are having trouble communicating in a biblical manner, I suggest you study and practice what the Word says about communication.

Dating is not having arguments about every small thing. Who wants a marriage about arguments all the time? Some arguments are too irrelevant in a relationship. Constant argument is not communication; it is fighting. A Christian dating should never get to the point of regular arguments or disagreement.

Complaining about everything your partner wants is not wise. Too much criticism about the ways of the other person means you are not satisfied with them. The continuous attempt of someone to correct every small mistake you make based on their opinion of how you should act, look, and dress in the dating period are signs of error. They are seeking a self-image they have built in their heads. They don't want you. You are not in dating if you are annoyed and dissatisfied with the ways of the other person. You have a choice to either get out of the dysfunction or continue fussing about your date.

No two individuals are exactly alike, and there will be misunderstandings. Several issues can prompt disagreements: spending habits, careers, entertainment, and family habits. Bickering can lead to resentment. But the key is to talk about the issues while dating.

Money and Power Isn't Everything

A major thing to discuss while dating is money. Financial issues have become a major part of the modern relationship and can sometimes lead to divorce in marriages. Having too much money or less money can both affect a relationship. Too much money available to spend can lead to ungodly choices, and less money can lead to stress.

Applying the process of the cross here is very important to avoid worldliness creeping into the relationship. Some have built a person of self with entertainment and worldliness, and if the person they have built is not placed on the cross, more arguments will emerge that question the Word of God. Knowing each other according to the cross and agreeing on certain things based on the Word is very important.

Money isn't the only thing to talk about while dating. It is important for couples to establish a healthy respect for one another.

Don't let lust blind you to ignore emotional abuse. Emotional abuse is serious. Looking down on others and treating them like your kids is another issue to be considered. Dating is not trying to train others about what you want them to be. It should be noted when the other person cares less about your personal and emotional issue and only cares about what they want.

My wife and I witnessed a married man once treating his wife in public as a child. We looked at each other and just shook our heads. One can clearly tell the relationship was based on power and control.

Power and control can lead to emotional abuse, and it blinds one to pride and arrogance to the point of not seeing and admitting wrong. No Christian should be dating anyone who can't see their own wrong. They will do wrong and will see no evil with their actions. They will not apologize or say "I am sorry that I am wrong" One thing I have learned to do is apologize when I am wrong. I apologize even to my kids. People who are not willing to learn, improve, or grow are problematic people.

What about Respect?

Someone who does not respect others might have problems respecting you. Respect is very important in a relationship. Respect is what a person is. If they don't have it, you can't teach them. Don't assume your responsibility in dating is to be a dad or mom of a toddler teaching them how to be respectful. There is nothing wrong about helping grown-ups acting like kids, but you should not date them because they are still kids in behavior. Many things combined contribute to what respect looks like.

Dating is not a period to bring the person of past relationships into the picture. The past has passed; move on. It is even crazy to compare your current relationship to your past or lamenting how unfair and bad you were treated by your ex to gain sympathy from your new date. Leave the past of self behind. Bringing the other persons of self in a relationship you are emotionally attached to is not dating at the cross, nor is it respectful.

Showing more emotional attachment to the opposite sex, flirting, and lusting after them is not dating at the cross. Although it is natural for a man or woman to be attracted to each other, once the choice is made to date, you should focus on the person you have decided to date. Do not give your partner a reason not to trust you. Once trust is lost in a dating period, the relationship must be broken. Loss of trust creates unhealthy jealousy.

Jealousy can be healthy because of love and unhealthy because of reason. God is a jealous God because we gave Him a reason to be jealous due to our unfaithfulness. Jealousy is a result of someone being suspicious of you and not trusting you. In most cases, people give others reasons for not trusting them. I don't think it is helpful to continue with dating someone if they give you clear reasons not to trust them. Most adult habits do not change overnight. Devoting your life to training an adult for dating is a waste of your life. A date is not your foster kid. But some are also jealous due to possessiveness or overprotectiveness which is unhealthy jealousy and can lead to aggressive behavior.

Experts would usually advise about regular aggressive behaviors, but do aggressive behaviors have to be regular before you make a decision? Remember, you are just in the dating period, and some decisions should be made instantly. Dating is not to nurture aggressive behaviors or anger management.

Certain behaviors in a dating period should send red flags. Some people grew up in an environment that believes beating and controlling women is natural. This belief is out of ignorance. In certain instances, both men and women can be aggressive toward each other. Things like manipulation, coercing, and intimidation is clearly against God's Word.

Don't put yourself in a position of restlessness and worrying about satisfying the other person to the point of losing your concentration of enjoying the life God gave you. If you are in the position of fear and intimidation, you are not in a godly dating relationship. You are in bondage. Abuse changes the status of any relationship to hostility. Hostility is not dating and should never be accepted.

Dating in fear of the other person is not dating at the cross. Hiding who you are and how you feel on the inside for fear of hurting or not losing the other person is self-imprisonment. Express who God has made you to be in all sincerity and truth. Freely express who you are and how you feel from within and be free. This will allow the other person the freedom to accept you or get out of the relationship. Don't be afraid to let people know when they have hurt you for fear of losing them. They are not the god of your life. Do not make those you date gods.

One thing I always admired about my wife is that she always told me that if I was not interested in her in the dating period, to just let her know anytime. She was a free woman because she already told me sex is not involved in the relationship from the beginning. I was either going to accept it or get out of it. When people are aggressive about pursuing sex in dating and are not willing to listen, it is not a good sign for a Christian relationship. But thank God, I accepted and have been blessed. When it comes to trust issues with my wife, there is nothing to worry about. I have always trusted her, and I always do. We do not need a DNA test to prove our kids are ours.

When Privacy and Behavior Changes Are a Problem

Privacy is a big issue with dating in both the world and the church. Privacy can also be a way for someone to hide destructive habits. If you happen to pick up the cell phone of a professing Christian you are dating and find serious ungodly images on it; you may need to consider ending the dating. Ending the relationship will help both of you. The other person will learn certain habits are not acceptable in a godly relationship, and you will free yourself from arguments and praying for deliverance. If you are dating someone and notice them trying to hide from you when answering phone calls, it indicates a huge problem. Another issue is trying to hide their family problems and baggage. What are they hiding? If you are in a Christian dating, you can't close all aspects of your life and call it your privacy. Defending hidden sin and calling it your privacy is toxic dating—not Christian dating.

Drastic or sudden changes in a dating relationship should not be taken lightly. If everything was going on fine and suddenly behavior changes that don't flow into oneness, then one has to ask "what changed?" Addressing this question is up to each individual because cach individual is responsible for bearing the consequences of their actions. Dating reaches a serious state when there is no longer peace with actions and character.

The death of spontaneous love and excitement should never be ignored. The love of God is so peaceful and spontaneous. It is not based on any self-image. People usually change drastically in a relationship of self. Spontaneous love from God does not change drastically in a manner that affects the other person.

There was a story in the news recently about a husband who murdered his wife and three kids for a relationship with a coworker. The wife ignored the behavior changes. She did her best to work things out, but the husband was never interested. The peace and joy of this beautiful woman with three kids were lost through no fault of her own.

What's in It for Me?

Looking at a relationship based on business and what profit could be generated from it is a sign of trouble which should not be ignored. Dating is not a career or commerce. Christian dating is an affair of the cross, not a racket. When people start saying within the dating period that "I did this for you; I did that for you but" then one should pay attention. They say "if you do this for me, I will do that for you" This sounds like a transaction, not a relationship.

Bargaining and negotiations are all signs of a toxic dating relationship. Business and entertainment dating where the focus is continuous desperation on fun can be toxic. Problems and blames emerge when the fun slows down. The fun seeker gets very uneasy and restless and will search somewhere else for more fun to feed self.

Our culture and society place much emphasis on the social aspect of dating while ignoring all other aspects. To the world, dating is going out to eat, watching movies, date nights, and doing fun things. There is nothing wrong with social aspects of dating if done within the boundaries of the cross. If social aspects of dating are self-satisfaction only, then the purpose of dating is lost. Self is addictive, never content, and wants the same thing over and over. Self wants to go out to eat every day when it can't afford it. Self wants to do what everyone is doing because they say it is fun.

You need to think about whether it is time to end the relationship if you are the only one dating yourself. Dating yourself means being the only one working to make the relationship a success because the other person is in self. Some people may value their career or another project above relationship or family. They show no balance and add no value to a relationship. This is the number one reason why extremely successful people fail in marriage. A relationship should have a full life on both sides if both individuals are in the path of the cross. If the other person is focused more on listening to friends above the Word of God, then the relationship may be toxic.

Feelings and perception of the other person based on intimate fun, and friendship can also affect a relationship. People have missed very good hardworking Christian people to date because they consider them non-intimate and fun. In a world where everyone desires to be entertained continuously, a good date may be missed. One has to know the other person to be close to them. They need to go past how they feel sometimes and try to know people from within. When worldly feelings of intimacy and fun are the focus of Christian dating, it may become toxic. People tend to miss the real person within because they are so focused on feelings.

Christian dating can become toxic when patterned according to the romance and intimacy issues of the world. The world places much emphasis on social, romance, and intimate issues. These issues are limited to the world and unlimited at the cross. Romance and intimate issues at the cross are spontaneous and unlimited. Intimacy at the cross is way higher than what the world has limited to the body. The world says bodily romance, bodily intimacy. The cross says unlimited romance and intimacy.

The love of the cross is not limited to the body only. True intimacy and romance are continuous and not limited to the body. Many things can be done in Christian dating to make you laugh, celebrate, and appreciate each other outside of the body. Yes! Christian dating and relationship can be fun. Be creative in pure holy intimacy and romance outside fornication in public - no privacy. If the other person cannot appreciate natural beautiful intimacy and romance outside of sex, then they may not be for you. Christian dating is not toxic, and toxic dating is never in line with God's Word. If it is toxic, get out of it. Don't let dysfunctional dating lead to marriage.

♥12♥
DESPERATION IN DATING

You have been at the path of the cross peacefully, and suddenly, you are being pressured to be with someone. You may not even know the type of family they are coming from, but they just want to marry you. "Marry me now," they say. "I am ready to settle down." Why the rush if you know nothing about them? Why the anxiousness? Didn't the Bible tell us not to be anxious for anything (Philippians 4:6)? It is good to allow God to prepare you for a relationship and dating. Desperate people can be very insecure, dominating, tyrannical, and just empty from within. Desperation is a sign of emptiness and void.

Being too desperate is an opportunity for Satan's blackout in the mind. A blackout mind can't see the truth or listen to anyone. I have seen singles so desperate they believe they can change grown-ups. Although the relationship may be clearly out of God's will, they will insist it's going to work. Desperate Christians need to stop assuming it is their responsibility to change others and make their way with self-power. Such thoughts are indications that one is still in self. Being too desperate to make things work that God clearly destined not to work would make it worse. Satan wants us to do what we like and does not want God to lead us.

Most singles have testified that God brought someone in their lives when they got tired of seeking a mate. God moved on their behalf when they stopped being crazy over the idea of getting married. They turned to the cross that calmed them down. God will always send someone once the heart is settled on the cross if it is His will for you to get married. Rely on God's will and don't force your will. Delight yourself in the Lord (Psalm 37:4).

It is a good thing to patiently wait on the counsel of God and allow Him to prepare us for life. We must be patient and allow it to work in us and our situation. Patience means period or time to be fulfilled. Desperation can prevent patience from finishing its work for us and our situation. Patience can show you things you would have missed in desperation. It would lead you to build character and your walk with God. As the apostle said: "But let patience have *her* perfect work, that ye may be perfect and entire, wanting nothing" (James 1:4).

Through the patience of not running to the altar, destructive and disturbing issues have been revealed in many cases. Most people have been thankful for waiting because waiting led them to decisions. Impatience and the rush to marry has led many to destructive marriages.

Physical attraction and attributes can also generate desperation. God placed the desire within humans to be naturally attracted to the opposite sex so that we can continue reproduction for life.

But He is a God of order and also has boundaries to follow. There is nothing one can do if people are desperate for marriage, but I will advise for those who want to go for it, they must go for it according to the knowledge of God. But let the distress and hopelessness, riskiness, and reckless that desperation reproduces be avoided. Let calmness rule your soul!

♥13♥
POWER, CONTROL, AND INTIMIDATION

Dating at the cross is not the nonsense "if you love me, do this or that for me" or "you really don't love me if you don't do this or that for me or with me." This type of behavior is manipulative and an attempt to control. Someone talking like this is not even at the path of the cross. They are not concerned about you. They are trying to manipulate you to get what they want.

A manipulator or abuser takes advantage of desperation. The manipulator comes with promises of filling every void in the victim's life. The victim gets excited and thinks they are in a good relationship, only to realize in the end they got nothing, but the manipulator gets everything. Desperation can lead to the catering of every desire whether righteous or unrighteous.

Dating is not working hard to seek attention, approval, and acceptance from the other person. People are so scared of missing out on someone they think is special for them and that if things do not turn out the way they expect, their world will fall apart.

Forcing or coercing to date or to be dated is wrong and is not biblical. It is abuse. Aggressiveness, temper tantrums, and restlessness should all serve as yellow warning lights that should quickly change to a stop light, meaning you have clear signs to end the relationship. These are all signs of self.

The cross demands denying self and taking up the cross. God will not tell you to do what is against His Word. Dating at the cross is not power, control, and intimidation of a child of God because such abusive practices are not supported by God's Word.

There are those who think they can have more voice in the relationship because of power and status which can also be manipulative and controlling. They want to use things and status as bait to get what they want. They forget that dating at the cross brings one to oneness. The cross cancels one's status, power, and authority. Leave your control, power, and pride at the cross if you want to date the Christian way. The way of the cross is humility.

Control and trust issues are a result of not being spontaneous in love. This is something that could be only achieved at the cross. The desire to control and dominate others is never Christian. The Bible never tells us to be transformed to the wimps of control freaks. The Word of God is against abusive lording over others.

Submitting yourself to control just to make people happy is submitting yourself to abuse. There is no control or coercing when synchronization occurs at the cross. The desires of self can lead delusional Christians to surrender to control and abuse. Get out of an abusive dating relationship, and it will cease to follow you. Dating should never be a curse but a blessing.

Let us try to act like our Father in heaven. God gave us free will and does not coerce or force us to choose or love Him, although He desires for us to love and choose Him. Christian dating is not coercing or forcing others to submit to our love requests. It is a problem to force the issue of love. Love must be spontaneous and not coerced. People must also take the initiative to serve God without coercion. People should not be forced to serve God so that they can be dated. If we are children of God, we will understand God's love is never forced or coerced.

♥14♥
DATING SINNERS IS DISOBEDIENCE

Dating unbelievers is not dating at the cross and is not doing what God wants. It is doing what you want and attempts to force God to bless a path that is not His. Unfortunately, several professing Christians pick out their own paths these days and expect God to make it His path. It is not God's will for His children to be in love with the devil.

Desiring the devil because one is handsome or beautiful, wise, and of good worldly status can be risky. Whether handsome or beautiful, a child of darkness is a child of darkness. Although God loves His children and sometimes can be merciful and gracious due to His sovereign ways, a risk is still a risk on our part. Satan is very wise in using his characteristics of beauty, merchandising, wisdom, music, entertainment, fashion, status, lust, greed, desire, passion, and trend to lure the children of God to date him.

The Bible is clear about children of the Spirit not dating children of the flesh. Children of the cross are prohibited from dating children of self. There is not much to be discussed about it. The Bible calls it disobedience:

Be ye not unequally yoked together with unbelievers: for what fellowship hath righteousness with unrighteousness? and what communion hath light with darkness? And what concord hath Christ with Belial? or what part hath he that believeth with an infidel? And what agreement hath the temple of God with idols? for ye are the temple of the living God; as God hath said, I will dwell in them, and walk in them; and I will be their God, and they shall be my people. Wherefore come out from among them, and be ye separate, saith the Lord, and touch not the unclean thing; and I will receive you (2 Corinthians 6:14–17).

It is deceptive for church singles to be in love with Satan and expect God to bless their relationship. They need repentance by asking God to forgive their sins, abandon their sin, and turn to God. Sin will not let go easily, but it must be intentionally dealt with through fasting and prayer. People in self will twist Scriptures to get what they want.

I understand it can be emotional and painful to break up an ungodly relationship. But if you are in the path of the cross and are obedient to it, then breaking an ungodly relationship should not be a problem. Not every Christian within the church has decided to follow Jesus. Dating someone who has not denied themselves and taking the cross daily and following Jesus is like dating Satan himself because self is the person of Satan or "I will." For example, before the fall of Adam to Satan, Adam was made of body, soul, and spirit (quickening of God). After the fall, Adam became soul (self), body, and spirit (dead). When the quickening power of God left Adam's spirit, all Adam had left was self.

Christians may be deceived to date someone in the path of Satan. For such deception to occur, the Christian following Christ must accept the ways of self to follow Satan. Several professing Christians within the church are still living in self and may not be ready for God's will for marriage. They need to grow in the path of Christ.

Being at different spiritual levels can also lead to potential conflicts in dating and marriage. Many within the church are opposed to fundamental biblical lifestyles regarding the relationship they want for themselves. They care less about righteousness or unrighteousness. They accepted Jesus but have not believed in righteousness (Romans 10:10). They believe partially. They believe in Jesus in theory but not in the lifestyle of the cross.

If the other person is not following Jesus, then to date them, you must leave the path of Christ, put down your cross, put on self, and follow Satan. In other words, you are returning to self just to date a child of Satan. People who are not following Jesus are following Satan. A Christian single in the path of the cross should pray not to drop the cross and return to self. Regardless of how nice ungodly people are, if they don't know Jesus, the Bible does not want you to date them.

Expect the unexpected when you date the devil. One thing you should expect in dating the unbeliever is lies and deception. If they don't know Christ, they have lying and deception within that you have no clue about. The choice to date a liar and a scammer is yours: "Ye are of your father the devil, and the lusts of your father ye will do. He was a murderer from the beginning, and abode not in the truth, because there is no truth in him. When he speaketh a lie, he speaketh of his own: for he is a liar, and the father of it" (John 8:44).

No one is more specialized in wooing people into deception than Satan. When you refuse the way of the cross, Satan can dazzle you with ways very difficult to detect. He can lead you into the fantasy of temporary happiness. He can deceive you the same way he did Eve as a master presenter: "But I fear, lest by any means, as the serpent beguiled Eve through his subtlety, so your minds should be corrupted from the simplicity that is in Christ" (2 Corinthians 11:3).

Most Christians fall into the temptation of dating an unbeliever because they say they are nice and caring. It is true there are many nice and caring people according to worldly standards. They are only nice based on what they want for themselves. But try to touch the deep self within them and see how nice they are. If they don't know Christ and have no intention of knowing Christ, you are deceiving yourself to date them.

God's concern about dating an unbeliever was that they would emotionally and affectionately draw your heart away from God. Someone who pulls your heart away from God is not from God. The Bible records several real-life scenarios where the people of God were influenced from God through marriage to pagans. Every commandment of God is good for our security and protection. God wants to protect you from the inside out. He understands that being damaged or destroyed from the inside will affect the outside. He wants you whole and not broken.

The Bible is plain and clear about not dating and marrying unbelievers. God has always separated people based on spirit and flesh. God not only commanded us to choose what He wanted for us, but He also made provisions of security and protection that comes with doing what He wants. If we go against God's will to date and marry an unbeliever, we are open without protections and security. I understand God's mercy, but why should we continue to take the risk of disobedience to His Word? That seems like being abusive to the relationship we have with God.

There are those who professed to be saved, which is a very good thing. But to be saved without making any effort to feed on the Word daily will lead to malnourishment and stunted growth. Some people are so malnourished to the point they are unable to take the cross in the dating period. Spiritual malnourishment leads to disobedience. They put little or no effort to study the Word. They may be an adult but babies in the Lord.

Spiritually, this can be compared to a pervert in the real world trying to date a baby. The baby is just a baby and wants to play around with other kids. The point I am trying to make is a lot of people within the church, or the body of Christ still do not know the basics of the cross about relationships. How can such a one be committed to a cross they have no idea of? It takes a long time for some people to move from one spiritual level to another. Is dating the place to learn the basics of the cross?

Many professing Christians have never committed to the cross. They never thought about the cross. They are biblically illiterate and perish for lack of knowledge. But they want a godly mate. When someone gets saved, they have to be taught the message of the cross. These days, people come to church to get stuff to feed the culture of self without any desire for the cross. Dating someone without any desire for the cross will affect your family and children if you happen to marry them by stubborn mistake.

Satan has worked very hard in creating a culture of self within the Christian community. The culture of self affects dating through disobedience to God's Word. Before we became Christians, most of us grew up feeding on the culture of self. The culture of self is designed to feed our souls. Dating involves emotions, energy, and a time investment that should not be wasted on the wrong person in self through our disobedience.

Family and social culture have a big influence on people. God wants to save you from ungodly dates and ungodly families. One has to decide to follow Jesus and put away bad family cultures or traditions. The cross will help get rid of the baggage. Sampson was a good example of the consequences and issues that can emerge out of dating unbelievers. The Philistine women were not going to abandon their ungodly cultures for Sampson. Ungodly people will turn your heart away for being dedicated to Christ.

We get into many problems when we turn our backs on God. I don't like divorce, but it happens. The problem also is people never learn, and most have taken divorce as a casual concept. Those who have been divorced for whatever reasons and are single again should make every effort to follow the path of the cross should they desire a relationship again. I am clearly talking about a relationship of the cross here. I am not talking about an abusive relationship where one is continuously harmed and tortured. It is not God's will for anyone to be subjected to abuse and torture. Being subjected to abuse is not dating or oneness.

Most people come from a background with ignorance of the Word and ways of God. They have no idea that God's concept of marriage is everlasting. The love of Christ brings us into a more perfect way. Let us ask God to strengthen us to follow the path of the cross and avoid unnecessary risks.

♥15♥
BREAKING UP A BAD DATING RELATIONSHIP

Thousands of people within the church want to marry but are not ready for marriage. Their perspective of marriage is fantasy, entertainment, and worldliness. All they want is the glamor that comes with standing at the altar and taking pictures to boast on social media. The rest is history.

Marriage is not to manage problems and baggage discovered in the dating period. The dating period is not a period of working out chronic problems of self either. The earlier you detect the problems and let go of the relationship, the sooner you will recover. Come on and be real! It is just a dating period. It is not your job to fix the chronic problems of self. I am not talking about simple things here, so don't take it to the extreme. You won't find a sinless, perfect individual on earth.

Signs from the Word of God are very clear and should not be ignored. The Word of God is Spirit and life, and it warns you about life. You can't find better advice anywhere in the world about your life than the Word. If you ignore the Word when you get hurt, remember the risk you took to get hurt. You can't ignore the Word and say, "I thought they were Christians" Sorry! Your thoughts are not the thoughts of God. If we perceive something wrong and went ahead to do it, then we are responsible to be honest enough before God to admit our issues and repent. Clear signs of a potentially bad relationship should never be ignored, suspended, or disregarded.

Naturally, it is not easy to break up a dating relationship where emotions and affections have been involved. But long term consequences of staying in a bad dating relationship are even more damaging and battering. A bad dating relationship is outside the path of the cross. This happens when a single individual or both individuals drop the cross and return to the ways of self.

There have been thousands of cases when people within the church ignored all promptings of the Holy Spirit and went with the deceitfulness of their hearts. Some were abused and seriously punished by self. Our disobedience to God and His ways is one reason why divorce and sin are so rampant within the church.

There are also other instances where people ignored warnings and got themselves in some serious issues that led to their death. Some Christians made the mistake of dating possessive, angry persons who later killed them as they wanted out. Some church folks have disregarded all sorts of warnings to marry people infected with sexually transmitted diseases within the church. They followed self because self seems to have it together. The devil lied to them, deceived them, and led them to death. Christianity is not just going to church; it is obedience to the cross.

Never get in the habit of disregarding small signs of trouble and dysfunctions. They will grow into monsters out of your control. Some have ignored clear small signs that became unexpected pop-up habits in a marriage. People usually have no idea of the nasty lifestyles people lived prior to their salvation, and some people who were never regenerated have the potential to quickly fall back into such habit without God's help. It is usually a big surprise when baby habits show up in a destructive adult form.

I have seen a very dedicated young man of God break up an engagement right within the church because the relationship was not God's will. Although people may think the person may be good for you, you have to consider if they are good according to the cross. Because this young man saw certain things of self in the other person that weren't of God, he was bold to break the relationship up. He saved himself from the self of the other person. He served very well as a leader within the kingdom of God. Guess what? God sent him a very beautiful, simple, and God-fearing and serving woman who was God's will for him. God's glory can be seen in their relationship in all aspects. They are both serving God in a mighty way.

Dating at the cross is discovering all aspects of self and denying them. It is better to have the courage to break up a relationship with self in control than to sit and wait for self-destruction. If you are in the bondage of a bad relationship, ask God to help you come out as soon as possible.

♥16♥
DATING IS NOT TRYING TO CHANGE PEOPLE

People do not change natural habits in a day. It is a process! This process of moving from the natural life to divine life is the work of God, not you. You can't change a person from the natural life to divine life so that you can date them. There are no human formulas as to when and how God does His work within us and how He wants to do it on our behalf or within those you wish to date. Your part is to pray for grace to strengthen your will to yield to God's will based on His sovereignty.

Growing in the divine life is based on accepting the ways of the cross. This is not something you can do for someone so that you can date them. You can't say "Baby, don't worry about your salvation, I am going to save you and give you a cross." They have to be saved on their own by repentance and believing in Jesus for the remission of their sins. You have no power to forgive the sins of your date.

It is our selfish human nature to assume or presume we are capable of changing others we are naturally attracted to. Satan wants us to live by the assumption of self and deny the established faith in God. It is always difficult to obey the Word of God when the wants of self overwhelm our soul. The Word of God, which should have supremacy in our souls, is lost as we drop the cross in exchange for what we want. It is a headache in trying to change people to make them what you want. Assuming the place of God is a dangerous thing. Why don't you wait on God to change them and bring them to you as a date? Why take a responsibility that is destined to fail?

The purpose of dating is not to transform or save others. You are not the Holy Spirit and can't provide salvation and sanctification to anyone. It is not anyone's job to deny or destroy the self of others. Neither is it anyone's job to force salvation on others because they desire them. The more the message of the cross is heard, the better the power of discernment. We can't set time frames for expecting others to change so that we can marry them.

A lot of people will come your way saying they know Jesus, but are they transformed from inside? Are they willing to take the cross and follow Jesus? Are they willing to sacrificially meet your needs at the cross?

One key reason dating at the cross is the best and will always be the best is God doesn't change, and His path establishes us. It is beneficial for us to take the cross and follow a path of establishment and stability: "For I am the LORD, I change not; therefore ye sons of Jacob are not consumed" (Malachi 3:6).

God is the only one with the ability to change people. Let us go to Him in humility and ask Him to change us from the headache we give ourselves in trying to change others. The Word of God is settled in heaven and does not change: "For ever, O LORD, thy word is settled in heaven" (Psalm 119:89). "I will worship toward thy holy temple, and praise thy name for thy lovingkindness and for thy truth: for thou hast magnified thy word above all thy name" (Psalm 138:2). Our job is to be obedient to the Word through the cross and not trying to do God's job of changing people.

♥17♥
POOR PREPARATION

In ancient cultures where marriages lasted for life, people prepared for marriage without even knowing the person they would marry. The preparation process led to the discovery of the prepared. The focus is on preparation, not arranged marriages.

It is pitiful that many young people within the church in dating relationships are not naturally and spiritually ready to settle. They are still within themselves. They talk big in self and expect this or that without being willing to pay the price of the daily cross. They stay in the vanity of the grave without the ability to resurrect their state of mind from the grave. There is no death, burial, and resurrection without the path of the cross. Many within the church aren't ready for a godly relationship, much less marriage.

We see very immature young folks rush to marry unprepared. Many neglect the opportunity of preparation in knowing God, developing a skill, pursuing an education, starting a business, and learning calmness in character, but they want a family. Some folks want a relationship, but have no divine plans for their lives and are going nowhere. From such, run away. They talk big but do nothing. They are useless in ministry and the world. Although God can change the useless and make them better, is it really your job to date the useless so that you can change them? What if they do not want to change? I advise you refer them to God so that God can work in them.

The psalmist encourages us to ask God to teach us to plan our time so we can live wisely: "So teach us to number our days, that we may apply our hearts unto wisdom" (Psalm 90:12). Someone in self has poor plans since they have not taken the cross to be taught of God. One has to be prepared to face life both in the world and church, and this applies to marriage as well. To properly prepare for marriage, one must wisely consider their spiritual and natural condition and that of their potential spouse.

Spiritual and Natural Readiness for Marriage

Isaac was a good example of a man ready for marriage both spiritually and naturally. Spiritually, Isaac knew God and naturally, he was wealthy. Joseph was ready for a relationship. He was spiritually mature and elevated in Egypt as one of the presidents. Rebekah and Ruth were ready for marriage. They were mature women who understood serving, caring, and loving. They supported and made their men greater.

The focus of spiritual and natural readiness has nothing to do with age (does not mean underage), physical looks, wealth, or a sense of humor. Dating life presents different challenges than marriage. Demands and values are affected by several circumstances, and one must recognize how these things demonstrate being prepared for marriage. When one is in self, changes in the dating period may affect faith.

A young adult who is spiritually and naturally settled may be more ready than a forty-year-old man with nothing and spiritually bankrupt. I am not promoting marrying the wealthy or most educated. I would be wrong doing so.

People should be prepared to meet at least the bare minimum necessary for a stable relationship. One who does not take care of his household is worse than an infidel as Scripture says: "But if any provide not for his own, and specially for those of his own house, he hath denied the faith, and is worse than an infidel" (1 Timothy 5:8).

A man must be spiritually mature to guide his family in the path of the cross, and the woman must also be spiritually mature to understand the guiding of the cross that secures sanctification of the household. Men or women who have little or no interest in the things of God will not raise a godly family. They will sit down and allow their toddlers to watch ungodly entertainment and say nothing because they are busy watching a movie themselves.

While dating, women tend to look at the tall and handsome; men and boys tend to look more at the beautiful woman. It is natural for a young man to be attracted to a young woman, but such attractions have to be put in perspective. Youthful focus on body attributes can be so intense to the point of not even considering things like responsibility, protection, and reason. They say we like each other until they find someone else who has more of the same qualities they have settled for. Their perspective on dating is basically personal satisfaction and not one ready for marriage.

Some youth usually fall into marriage early for reasons like "he makes me laugh, or she makes me laugh" For real? Is comic the only reason for marriage? What happens when problems arise? Would jokes solve problems?

People usually want to rush into marriage without knowing someone or their background. The culture and background of people influence how they think and act. Be curious to know who is the father and mother of your date. Watch them closely and how they react to godly issues and family. What are their values? Are they simple? Are they full of drama? Can you put up with their excessive wordiness and materialism? Are they involved in serving the Lord? These are questions to ask. Meeting someone and just dating them without any attempt to know their faith or family is just simple crazy.

The culture that entertainment dating has created and formed is not biblical. The entertainment dating is meeting someone in the street or a bar and based on physical appearance and assumes they are good for you. A decision is made on the spot. Such instances are based on self and lust as the relationship ends when the demons arise. Professing Christians in self have fallen so many times to hard realities as they drop the preparation of the cross, put on the desperation of self, and do what they want. They gave themselves unnecessary trouble.

Spiritual Preparation

One of my greatest regrets in life is poor spiritual preparation. Poor spiritual preparation can affect the way we do things. I was told that if you are smart in school, talented, or work hard, you can be successful. There is nothing wrong with hard work and smartness, but preparation in the path of the cross should be elevated above all.

I did not grow up in a spirit-filled or Pentecostal church. I grew up in the midst of mixed religions, and God has to reveal to me that the path of the cross is the right path. It pains me too much to see the lack of spiritual and natural preparation of young people within churches for life and relationships. Teaching our kids that success is going to college or being a businessman only is a half-truth. Our children need to be taught at a young age how to pursue excellence in everything.

Daniel and his friends were chosen to stay in the palace because they were prepared intellectually and spiritually. One should have the same drive for spiritual success as they do for natural success. Faith without works is dead.

Get out of self, take your cross, and allow Jesus to teach you— Jesus is willing to teach you in the path of the cross. He wants you to reach the joy He has set before you: "But the Comforter, which is the Holy Ghost, whom the Father will send in my name, he shall teach you all things, and bring all things to your remembrance, whatsoever I have said unto you" (John 14:26). Be like Mary who sat in the path of Christ to be taught. Christ will lead you to make the right choices (Luke 10:39–42).

Running from conference to conference for information without having Christ within will do you no good. Let your inner being be your classroom for the Holy Spirit to teach you. "What man is he that feareth the Lord? him shall he teach in the way that he shall choose" (Psalm 25:12). Give yourself to the path of the cross and to be taught by the cross. The teachings and preparation of the cross will lead you to joy and peace: "And all thy children shall be taught of the LORD; and great shall be the peace of thy children (Isaiah 54:13).

♥18♥
KNOWING SOMEONE

Let us be clear that just because you are a Christian, it doesn't mean you can just marry anyone who professes to be a Christian. Every single Christian is not in the path of the cross, and most professing single Christians are deeply in love with themselves. They love the world, the lust of the flesh, the pride of life, and the lust of the eyes.

As long as one is in the path of the cross, there is no need to worry about knowing if the other person is as well. The revelation of each other takes place at the path of the cross. God has to bring people together in oneness of His will. That is His job, not yours. The oneness of God surpasses compatibility and chemistry as the world intends. God has to create a perfect union of two people becoming one. Both parties will usually know when this happens. God will reveal to the single man the right time to approach and make known his intent to a single woman, and the single woman will also know how to respond based on confirmation in her spirit. This knowing is from God.

Naturally, no two people are the same. This means both individuals can be in Christ, but it may not be God's perfect will for them to unite as a couple. God will cause one or both parties to know whatever the outcome will be. There will be perfect peace in either case.

If either or both people decide to get together for selfish reasons, it will also be revealed. Going around in the flesh or self claiming another person as your mate is foolishness. Let God do it. Let it flow, and you will cease from much effort of the flesh. I am not God and will not give you a formula for this or that. Stay in the path of the cross and let spontaneous love flow. It may be sooner or later.

God can reveal several things to you about your date if you are in the path of the cross. God knows and sees everything you can't see about your date. He knows what they are hiding from you. He knows their deepest secrets you don't even know about. He knows what they do when you are not around. He knows whether they have what it takes to reach complete oneness at the cross. God can show you all indicators according to His will to see whether they could achieve oneness.

Sometimes because God loves you so much, He can point out things based on practical Christian virtues. I am not talking about the cause and effect promoted by the world. I am talking about a life that is led by Christ and belongs to God. The most important thing is denying self, taking the cross, and following Jesus. He hears, sees, and knows the future.

Knowing someone is not a formula. There is no particular method or steps to take in meeting or knowing someone. The methods and steps of the world can sometimes be disastrous. No follower of Christ should be going to a bar, club, or worldly events just to meet someone. The best place to know someone is at the path of the cross. We take the cross for the purpose of knowing Jesus, and the only way to know

Jesus is to follow Him. As we continually follow Him, we learn His divine attributes.

When we follow Jesus, we really have no idea where we are going. Jesus knows where we are heading because He is in the lead. This is quite different from the world which says you should know what you want through mental expectations and go after it for yourself. The world's method of trying to know someone is completely external and sinfully exploring. It is usually instant gratification as self-attempts to feed on the flesh in the name of romance. In the end, self temporarily gets its way that leads to the death of the relationship. People are broken and hurt when things fall apart. "Every good gift and every perfect gift is from above, and cometh down from the Father of lights, with whom is no variableness, neither shadow of turning" (James 1:17).

I never emphasize the need for a formula or steps to knowing someone at the path of the cross because God is sovereign, meaning He can do anything He wants to do. However, there are a few examples in the Bible about meeting and knowing someone. Meeting and knowing someone may involve both male and female interactions and associations.

- Ruth met Boaz through simple loving kindness and service.
- Rebekah met Isaac through the service of loving kindness.
- Sampson went to the wrong place to meet ungodly women.

Let me begin with church single women by saying this: learn to be nice to decent, godly single men within the body of Christ. Why don't you offer to help them serve God sometimes? Why don't you bake a cake as a gift for their service to God? The same goes for young men. Young men should not be afraid to ask single women in the path of the cross out. Lovingkindness should not be done in the flesh by expecting something in return. Be nice and expect nothing in return. Who knows what will come out of your niceness?

Rebekah never knew a marriage would come out of her kindness and service to Abraham's servant. Sometimes, your kindness can refer you to someone better than your expectation. This was what happened to Rebekah. Her kindness to Abraham's servant was a setup for her Isaac. Interactions of kindness are one way to meet and be open to others. Learn to be kind to singles at the cross. You never have an idea what will come out of it.

Christian kindness is not binding. Let others be free. Being nice and kind without cause opens a door for interactions. Never be afraid of rejection as you offer kindness and never expect obligations. You may be kind to people but may not be the right fit for them, and you should accept and understand that.

We all understood Sampson's trouble as he attempted to know the ungodly. He was used and defeated in his pursuit for them. Knowing someone is not a fixed formula. It is being open to what God wants to do in your life through kindness as directed. Learn to flow with God, and you will be safe. Never have in your mind that if you keep buying things for a female, you can get them, or if you keep baking cake for a man, you can win them as well. Be free to do as God wills—learn spontaneous kindness and interaction like Ruth, Boaz, Rebekah, and Isaac, and you will be fine. Don't rush to make any decision until you get to know people. Dating is not a high-speed race.

♥19♥
LIFETIME DATING

God does not change. His loving kindness doesn't change at all. His eternal spontaneous love at the cross is the same every day and any time. This is a joy the world does not guarantee. It flows from within all the time. The spontaneous love of God at dating is the same in marriage. This should motivate Christians to believe God will have mercy on us for a mate in the path of the cross and thus avoid much headache and pain in the search for love. Love through the cross is always joy.

No person on earth is more romantic and spontaneous than our great God. It just takes years and years for most of us within the church to understand the fullness of God's love. God is full of all the love we need. If only self gets out of the way, the affection of love full of life can flow on a daily basis until we die. Love is the theme of the elevated life.

As we settle in the path of the cross during the dating period and become established in the path of the cross, we find ourselves dating continuously. Why? Because the cross unites us to God's unchangeable love. The love of God in dating is not different from His love in marriage. Jesus understands human nature and the ever-changing demands of the flesh. That is why He requires us to take the cross daily. The same way the cross is taken daily at the dating period is the same way it should be taken in marriage.

The only way to experience and practice dating at the cross daily in marriage is to continuously follow Christ without interruption. The original Greek meaning of the word follow means to always be in the presence of the person being followed.[xvi] The purpose of following was to develop features that resemble the leader or the person being followed. We follow Jesus to look like Him, behave like Him, and be like Him. We seek to know His mind and understand Him.

The daily cross is the livelihood of the spiritual life. Just as food and water are necessary for our daily physical subsistence, so is the daily cross. Christ gives us this daily bread for the spiritual person to develop and manifest in love. Jesus is the daily bread because He is the Bread of Life (John 6:35). He is the living waters (John 4:10). The daily cross provides the basic necessities for the life of our spirits. Our spirit needs food daily to grow, and the food we need is the daily cross. It comes from Christ who feeds us daily, but believers are supposed to seek Christ daily. The basic necessities for our daily life at the cross will never run out.

Dating at the cross is said to be lifetime when it leads to oneness at marriage because it is elevated above all forms of dating. If people follow the principle of the cross continuously and recognize God's love, then marriages at the path of the cross will experience the same joy of dating "Until death do us part" Dating at the path of the cross is the only dating that lasts a lifetime.

However, some naysayers question if Christian dating is supposed to be for life by asking why Christian marriages and relationships fail. The answer is simply self. It is the self of either person or the self of both dropping the cross. Again, self is simply the self-centered life and is never a sacrificial life.

The more I seek God, the more I have grown to love my wife and children. Life at the cross is just a beautiful, unexplainable thing. The joy that comes from the sacrifice of the cross is found only in the path of following Christ. This overflowing life and joy are carried daily from dating to marriage. The love obtained from being crucified with Christ does not stop at dating before marriage. This joy in dating the Christian way flows continuously until death. True Christian dating continues before and during marriage because dating at the cross is continuous.

Continuous dating is possible when dating at the cross leads to marriage. Marriage is never meant to kill the excitement of dating. Marriage should amplify the excitement of dating. Marriage comes with new challenges as two become one, but the joy of dating that comes out of the resurrected life should be enough to balance the issues a couple will experience. One can be joyful in the midst of challenges because the joy of the cross gives peace not obtained from the world.

If your dating at the cross leads to marriage, remember to take the cross daily and encourage each other to take the cross as given by Christ daily to keep the joy. Sometimes, the process may involve endurance and despising shame to get to the joy, but we must be willing to follow the path of the cross because that is the only guaranteed path for the fullness of joy. Don't let marriage stop you from dating your spouse.

The love of God is the same all the time. Change of status doesn't change the spontaneous, loving kindness experienced at dating. We can flow in the love of God as long as we continually pursue staying in the presence of God.

♥20♥
THE MYSTERY OF ONENESS

The goal of Christian dating is oneness in God's will. Perfect oneness in God's will is exclusive to God and is a mystery to the world. The concept of oneness in dating is completed in marriage as two become one.

The world wonders how a male and female can become one person. The world also has a problem understanding that the Father, Son, and Holy Ghost are one. They question how three persons can be one. This is something science can't explain either. They try to figure out the math that three units put together is not one but three. That is why the concept of oneness is not for the unbeliever or the world because their eyes are still closed. They can't see what we see or understand what we understand. Professing Christians who have not denied self or taken the cross might not understand the mystery of oneness as well. But oneness should be the goal of Christian dating.

The apostle Paul called the oneness that joins a male and a female in marriage a great mystery: "For this cause shall a man leave his father and mother, and shall be joined unto his wife, and they two shall be one flesh. This is a great mystery: but I speak concerning Christ and the church" (Ephesians 5:31–32). Oneness is spiritual and flows from within. The oneness of God is the source of spontaneous love. It flows from within and flows all over an individual.

Throughout Scriptures, the spiritual principle of oneness is emphasized. Oneness is required for a healthy individual, a healthy church, and for nature itself to function correctly. Humans were created to operate in oneness, but sin brought division within us.

There was no striving of disarray, lawlessness, or pandemonium within Adam's soul before he fell. His soul was in a quickened state of oneness. The body, soul, and spirit were in complete unity. Our body, soul, and spirit were created to operate as one unit. Because of sin, our soul divided itself from the Spirit of God that existed within our spirit. If we are not in Christ, we are divided within ourselves.

A Christian who dates an unbeliever is dating a divided person pulled in every direction as the soul refuses to answer the call of the Spirit toward God. God the Father, God the Son, and God the Holy Spirit are one: "I and My Father are one" (John 10:30 NKJV), and this oneness is also seen in creation and numerous supporting verses. God the Father, the Son and Holy Spirit are one (Genesis 1:26). In Christ, the fullness of God is one. "For it pleased the Father that in him should all fullness dwell" (Colossians 1:19). The church and Christ are one. Believers are one in Christ.

A male and a female are one in marriage. Understanding the oneness of God creates a picture that supports why the goal of Christian dating should be oneness. Let us not confuse ourselves with oneness based on physical units or substance as many are still confused with the concept of the Trinity—which is simply one God in three persons.

In oneness, love overflows and the couple consider each other in everything they do. You will hear them say, "I need to talk to my wife or husband about it," As we get closer to God, we are concerned about how God feels about everything we do because He is within us, and we are in His presence always. Two individuals become one by being one with God first through the cross. They become one with God by becoming whole within themselves at salvation. This oneness in God's will should not be misunderstood that humanity is part of the Trinity. The mystery of oneness should be spiritually discerned and understood.

The process of Christian dating involves self-denial, cross taking, and following Jesus. It is Jesus who directs the path of a dating relationship. It is Jesus who makes the path through which spontaneous love flows. All we need to do is follow, and He will direct our paths: "In all thy ways acknowledge him, and he shall direct thy paths" (Proverbs 3:6). Dating in the path of the cross is being one with Christ, and we will want to court someone who is also one with Christ.

Oneness over Compatibility Or Chemistry

It would be a great risk to move from dating to marriage if oneness in God's will could not be achieved at the dating period. Close attention should be paid to the aspect of oneness with God. Both parties become one as each person becomes one with God, in God's will. Oneness meets both social and spiritual demands.

Satisfaction and fulfillment in the dating period can only be found at the cross. The goal of dating at the cross is not compatibility or chemistry but oneness in divine life. At the cross, the warfare between the many persons brought by self into a dating relationship and its never-ending demands are put to death and buried. When all parties involved in dating deny the never-ending wantonness, craziness, deception, lust, and drama of self, divine life emerges to form an experience of oneness.

God's system talks more about oneness than compatibility. Oneness provides spontaneous and synchronized love that chemistry and compatibility can't fulfill. Compatibility and chemistry are external and deals with the natural standards of the flesh. They deal with benchmarks set by the wisdom of men to match expectation.

God does not deal with people based on the measurements and standards of the world. What the world considers compatible and chemistry, may not be uniting. Compatibility and chemistry do not create the oneness the cross provides.

Just because you love football and someone else love football, doesn't mean you are compatible or have chemistry. What happens when one stops liking and watching football with you? Although you may be like-minded in external things, you may be divided within if cross taking is one-sided. A lot of Christians are making the mistake of dating people who are not in Christ because they may be in the same professional field or like the same movies. It is always advisable to wait than to rush into things where oneness does not exist.

Self-accomplishments or status does not lead to oneness. What happens when self is dated is that one's entire life is spent in meeting the continuous demands, wantonness, and standards of self. The relationship becomes rocky or even fails if the demands of self are not met.

It is not possible to be in oneness and have communication or chemistry issues. At oneness, communication is good. Some at the cross have been married for forty, fifty, and over sixty years to one person. Although they were not perfect in oneness, they believed in the oneness of God's will. They believe in oneness by faith. How much more if they were perfect in oneness?

Compatibility or chemistry is generally about you liking what he or she likes. If compatibility is based on just likeness of emotional or sensual things, what happens when those things are taken away? What happens when the emotions of the flesh disappear, or the excitement disappears? Compatibility and chemistry fail when things liked together changes. Both people may like the same things in dating, but the love for those things they liked during the dating period may change.

Everything should fall in the place of oneness. The goal of following Christ is to be one with Christ. We should be united within us in body, soul, and spirit. We are said to be at peace within if our body, soul, and spirit are in unity. Self separates the unity of body, soul, and spirit. The goal of a Christian relationship is oneness and not man-made compatibility and chemistry benchmarks. Time has to be spent at the cross if you want to meet someone at the cross.

As long as each person in the relationship takes the cross on a daily basis, the relationship stays within oneness. This is where the world gets it wrong as compatibility and chemistry fails. People who might have been compatible in the beginning according to worldly measurements quickly find themselves apart due to the slightest change of compatibility components. Choose oneness in God's will over compatibility or chemistry.

When two people meet at the cross, love is spontaneous. There are no complex issues. Issues only show up if one or both parties drop the cross. The cross is the only place where oneness is achieved. In oneness, everything flows. In a true Christian relationship, there are no formulas, programs, or steps. Oneness in love is way elevated above compatibility and chemistry.

As the apostle elaborated on the oneness of marriage: "So ought men to love their wives as their own bodies. He that loveth his wife loveth himself. For no man ever yet hated his own flesh; but nourisheth and cherisheth it, even as the Lord the church" (Ephesians 5:28–29). In oneness is the full page of everything one desires in a marriage. There is no need to worry about intimacy and social issues. The spirit of oneness covers both spiritual and physical things.

♥21♥
GET IN WHOLE, CONTINUE, OR COME OUT WHOLE

The way of the cross is the best preparation for a dating relationship. The cross prepares you to get into a dating relationship whole, continue in it whole, or come out of it whole if it doesn't work. Outside of the cross, there is no guarantee of getting into a dating relationship whole and coming out of it whole.

It is sad that most people get into a dating relationship in a broken state and come out of it more broken. Some get into it in a state of wholeness and get out broken if it doesn't work. The reason for this brokenness is people venture into a relationship with self alive and not passing through death, burial, and resurrection. Satan is carried into a relationship when self is carried into it as well.

It is natural for people to get hurt after spending time and emotions in a relationship that failed. Although it is possible to get hurt, if one stayed in the path of the cross—meaning the will of God— they can come out of a failed dating relationship whole because the cross never fails.

In a relationship, one can be hurt in several ways because they invested time and emotions. The best way to approach dating is to expect nothing from anyone. Let people prove themselves in the oneness of Christ, and if you are one with Christ, you can operate in oneness of Christ in the dating period. Even if dating doesn't work, you are still a winner if you follow the principles of the cross. Yes! Christians too can be hurt, and the hurt can be painful. The key here is if dating does not work, the hurt should not last long.

The hurt usually lasts long when a Christian chooses to treat dating as marriage and breaks every boundary of God's Word. We always create our own miseries and, for the most part, we have no one to blame. We can't complain about the other person when we never followed the will of God in the first place. It is never the responsibility of the other person to make us live for God. It is our choice and risk if we live for a date rather than live for God. Let us learn to give to God only those things reserved for Him.

The oneness of marriage should not be given in dating. Although you can operate in oneness in the dating period because you are one with Christ, being in oneness with God's will means staying within the boundaries God has set and defined in a dating period. Christians in self who are not in oneness with God's will usually hurt the most when a dating relationship doesn't work.

A Christian should fight not to embrace the deception of worldly romance in the flesh that love is giving your body at will to the other person. Giving your entire body, soul, and spirit in the dating period is giving up your entire life to someone who has not committed to the oneness of marriage with you. Dating in oneness should be limited to soul and spirit, not handing over your body.

Although spontaneous affections in soul and spirit can flow naturally with the best fit, it should still be limited as required by God's Word. I understand we are all humans and sometimes we need to show affections in small things like holding hands, hugging in public, or greetings with a kiss in public, but avoid being naked or in isolated places.

One respect I have for my wife is she was never desperate to give me her nakedness. She told me up front that sex is not involved. I had to pursue her. Her character, family kindness, and caring were enough to win me. She is not a perfect human being as none of us are, but she is perfect for me. Showing a man or woman naked bodily romance is not oneness in dating.

Some people get so hurt by assuming responsibilities in the dating period they are not required to fulfill. Some invest too much in the other person in an attempt to buy their love. This is a dangerous state to be in. Dating has a limit, and when one goes outside that limit, they are bound to be hurt. It is common these days for people to say, "I did this or that for them, but they left me for another person." If you want to show kindness to the other person with gifts, give it freely. Do not attempt to bind others with objects of kindness. Allow people to love you freely. Learn to do simple things without being too extravagant because no man can buy the love of the cross. Let dating flow spontaneously in the will of God.

Christian dating has boundaries or limits. Without boundaries or limits, it would not be Christian dating. God set boundaries or limits for our protection and security. If we cooperate with God's plan for our lives, we will have fewer headaches.

The way of the world provides ongoing headaches and drama. It is false Christianity to listen to the world's advice and follow its ways and expect God to bless it. No one expects a relationship to fail. But not all dating relationships are according to God's will. Be humble enough and willing to accept God's counsel if someone is not for you. It is better to get out of a dysfunctional dating relationship than to blindly proceed in a trapped dysfunctional marriage. Failed marriages start at the dating period. So, prepare to get into dating whole and come out whole if things do not work out. I pray the grace of God will keep you within His limits during the dating process.

♥22♥
MEETING AT THE STATE OF THE CROSS

To meet at the cross, one has to leave self behind. You must leave self behind, and the person you date must do the same. Dating at the cross is when two individuals practicing self-denial meet at the cross. Both individuals are doing the best they can with the power of grace to deny self and accept God's will for their lives. Each individual practices the experience of death, burial, and resurrection in Christ on a daily basis and in all situations. As self is denied, the cross is taken, and life is powered by resurrection power. There is no pressure or anything to worry about since dating is run by a life from above. Everything flows in a spontaneous manner even in times of trouble or challenge.

The central theme of the daily cross is allowing the power of grace through the power of the resurrection to work in us. It takes the power of grace to strengthen our will to be responsive to what God has done for us. As the resurrection power fuels our will through grace, we receive strength to deny self, take the cross, and follow Christ.

Our duty in allowing Christ to lead us is: follow! In the world, following someone is seen as weakness. But following Christ makes our weakness become our strength. "And he said unto me, My grace is sufficient for thee: for my strength is made perfect in weakness. Most gladly therefore will I rather glory in my infirmities, that the power of Christ may rest upon me" (2 Corinthians 12:9). The power of Christ is only found in the path of the cross. It is this power that protects a godly dating relationship and provides the same continuity of joy in dating to marriage at the cross.

The path of the cross is the way, the truth, and the life. It is not a path of deception, tricks, and games. It is a serious path. At the path of the cross where self is absence, Satan is unable to trick you because Jesus is in front of you and leading you. Jesus will show you things you can't see. Yes, He will show you deep hidden things you need to know to make an informed decision. Jesus will make it clear to you whether someone is good for you or not.

There will be overwhelming peace when two cross-bearers and selfless people meet. Jesus knows your need and desires, and there is no need to include self in making a long list. Jesus is not only concerned about your spiritual need, but He is also concerned about your social and emotional needs as well: "Delight yourself in the LORD, and He will give you the desires of your heart" (Psalm 37:4 ESV). As you reckon to be dead with Christ, buried with Christ, and resurrected with Christ, you come out a new person by faith and Jesus meets all your needs by faith: "But my God shall supply all your need according to his riches in glory by Christ Jesus" (Philippians 4:19).

♥23♥
THE FULLNESS OF JOY

If your life is empty, don't expect a human to fill it up. A life can only experience fullness and satisfaction in the presence of God. Unsatisfied people continuously want this or that. Their wants never stop because they are not content in God. They are always searching for the good, better, or best. Looking for good or better qualities in humanity based on self-satisfaction is deceptive.

The Bible talks about the heart as being very deceptive and not to be trusted. As Bernard clearly puts it: "Every rational person naturally desires to be always satisfied with what it esteems to be preferable. It is never satisfied with something which lacks the qualities it desires to have. So if a man has chosen a wife because of her beauty, then he will look out with a roving eye for more beautiful women. Or if he is desirous of being well dressed, he will look out for even more expensive clothes, No matter how rich is he, if wealth is his desire, he will envy those who are richer than he is."[xvii] If they seek satisfaction in status, then they will always seek higher status than their choosing.

A big problem with searching for satisfaction in natural or outside qualities can lead to a dangerous road of constant searching and dissatisfaction because there is never satisfaction in natural or physical objects. And when you aren't satisfied with a person, you will feel empty. Emptiness in a dating relationship will lead to potential problems in a marriage.

Satisfaction does not come from the preference of self. It comes from the denial of self and taking the will of God. God can satisfy one's choosing. Satisfaction is a divine choice, not a natural choice: "And the LORD shall guide thee continually, and satisfy thy soul in drought, and make fat thy bones: and thou shalt be like a watered garden, and like a spring of water, whose waters fail not" (Isaiah 58:11).

Enjoying the fullness of joy in the presence of God prevents you from making several mistakes and gives you the wisdom to sense and end a bad relationship on time without delay. In His presence, God shows you the path you should take and will help your decision-making process: "Thou wilt shew me the path of life: in thy presence is fullness of joy; at thy right hand there are pleasures for evermore" (Psalm 16:11). But we must first learn how to seek God's presence and experience the daily cross.

Practicing and experiencing the daily cross should never be made into a formula. We should seek to know God by faith and by faith alone. God is faithful to perform His Word when it comes to our relationship with Him. If we develop a heart for Him, He is there. He comes to form an effortless relationship with us and shows us how to spontaneously love Him without much effort.

Brother Lawrence came to develop a very conscious relationship with God to the point of being able to recall his spirit whenever it went astray from God's presence. As he said,

> This exercise was rather difficult. Yet, I was able to continue it without being disturbed when I was involuntarily distracted.

It occupied as much time during my regular working day as it did in my prayer time. At all times—every hour and every minute—I drove everything out of my spirit that might take me from the thought of God. This has been my everyday routine since I began my walk with the Lord. Although sometimes I practice it timidly and with a great many mistakes, I am still quite blessed by it 53."[xviii]

The presence of God is the practice of divine life from heaven. God wants His divine life to become natural to us. Following fixed and scheduled programs can cause us to miss the spontaneous love and care of God's presence. We do not serve God based on scheduled love and time management. Just imagine if when God called Moses, he replied by telling God it wasn't his devotion time yet.

As we get accustomed to the presence of God, we understand our purpose in life. Practicing the presence of God in our daily activities can lead us to know God better rather than depending on worldly advice on relationships and dating. No amount of talent, skill, intellect, or knowledge is required to get in the presence of God. Stepping in the presence of God only requires a willing and faithful heart.

Moses asks God to assure him His presence will be with him in doing what God required. He understood the failure in dealing with people without the presence of God. "And he said, 'My presence shall go with thee, and I will give thee rest.' And he said unto him, 'If thy presence go not with me, carry us not up hence'" (Exodus 33:15). I believe one reason God used Moses the way He did was Moses knew God as God. He understood the ability of God and the limitation and failure of man. Moses' response to God is always "I can't, but You will."

It is not possible to spend time in God's presence without being filled with love. Learn to live a full life at the dating stage. Refuse the deception of Satan to empty your life with the thoughts you are not complete because you are single. A cross-taking single Christian is complete with or without a date. It is not the job of a date to fill you with the fullness of joy that comes with being in God's presence.

God knows our desires and the best fit for us. There is no need to be anxious about not having who we prefer as a partner or mate. Let us give our preference to the cross and let God work things out for us.

Isaac never met Rebekah. He had no idea Rebekah was very beautiful. Prayer was not only answered, but answered according to Isaac's desire. Rebekah was the full package of beauty and service. Isaac did not go around looking for a beautiful woman. A beautiful woman with the heart of a servant was brought to him.

Go to God, and He will bring you what you want: "Delight thyself also in the LORD; and he shall give thee the desires of thine heart" (Psalm 37:4). God knows exactly what you want and what can satisfy you: "For he satisfieth the longing soul, and filleth the hungry soul with goodness" (Psalm 107:9). Do you want to be satisfied at all times? Then desire a burning passion for going after God. Act like you need and want God. Chase Him, and He will satisfy you whether you are in pain or pleasure. Yes! He will.

Being in the presence of God during the dating period gives much joy and rest. Dating will be meaningless and full of burden without the joy of the Lord, and the joy of the Lord can only be experienced by staying in the presence of the Lord. We can never be satisfied if our desires do not match God's. Complete satisfaction comes from seeing things as God sees them. One should be satisfied in God before settling down for a relationship.

♥24♥
WAITING ON GOD

The reason for a Christian to wait on God is for His counseling. Although His counsel is also found in His Word, it is necessary to wait on confirmation with His purpose. We wait on God's counsel to deliberate with Him so that His Word fits our purpose before we act. God's chosen people in the Old Testament had a big problem with waiting on God: "They soon forgat his works; they waited not for his counsel: But lusted exceedingly in the wilderness, and tempted God in the desert. And he gave them their request; but sent leanness into their soul" (Psalm 106:13–15). It is very easy and common to read into Scripture what we want out of it.

In today's world, God's people have made it a habit of going to Him only after they have followed their own ways and minds and failed. The Bible clearly tells us there is always a way that looks like the right way to people, but in the end, it leads to their destruction (See Proverbs 14:12 and 16:25). The word counsel means to advise and deliberate. The lust for what we want is the reason we are unable to wait on God. Again lust comes from self. We want what we want for ourselves right now.

Let us always remember that self is of the devil. The devil is not patient. He rushes and insists on what he wants right away. Self insists on seizing the opportunity of the fleshly cravings. Being in a hurry and restless state is something to watch out for. The excitement and boldness to let everyone know you have a new unsaved boyfriend or girlfriend may be short-lived. One reason the devil rushes you is for you to forget what God has done and what He is capable of doing for you. The devil wants you to rush to accept his second best. You may like the second best, but it may not be God's best for you.

The problem of God's people in the wilderness was desperation in difficult times. They bothered God for what they wanted and refused to wait on His best. God gave them what they were desperate for, and their ungodly appetite brought them trouble. Most of them got sick and died of their desires.

How many times have we settled on God's second best and refused to wait on Him? Some Christians have lost their lives by marrying people in the church with sexually transmitted diseases. God would have shown them the issues had they waited. The purpose of waiting on God is for God's counsel. God knows and wants what is best for you. Naturally, waiting is not easy, but if we purpose in our hearts to please God, He will strengthen us as the psalm advises: "Wait on the LORD: be of good courage, and he shall strengthen thine heart: wait, I say, on the LORD" (Psalm 27:14).

Let us learn to wait on God and work on self-denial while we wait. God will reveal the self in us that we must deal with in the waiting period. Isaac did not go out looking for a mate like Samson did. Sometimes waiting can be like being in a place of a horrible pit— it can be like being in the grave where everything seems to be dead.

That is exactly the purpose of the cross to bring us to the place where life is no longer about us but God.

Self is dead at waiting, buried and resurrected into God's will. Again, hear what the psalmist says about the working of resurrection power to bring you back out of the grave: "I waited patiently for the Lord; and he inclined unto me, and heard my cry. He brought me up also out of an horrible pit, out of the miry clay, and set my feet upon a rock, and established my goings" (Psalm 40:2).

Those who wait on the Lord may face several challenges and sometimes pressure from relatives and church members, they will say "why are you still single? When am I going to have a daughter or son-in-law or when am I going to have a grandchild" Really? Don't you recognize self and Satan in all these? These are all crazy wild spirits of self. Such know nothing about God's sovereign ways. They do not know the future; they can't even help themselves and want to help others.

The society, environment, culture, and media influences waiting on God. Some Christians prefer expert advice rather than God's counsel and end up being more confused. God has guaranteed for those who are patient on waiting on Him that He will establish their paths. He will place their feet on a rock. He will ensure they walk in a straight path and secure their steps. God takes His time to prepare those who wait on Him

Waiting on the counsel of the Lord is allowing God to prepare you for His best. God searches within you for self that may be a hindrance. In the long run, God teaches you how to learn to deny the self you so deeply love. Nothing is lost during the waiting period on the Lord. In the waiting period, God renews you through resurrected life. You gain a new life you never expected.

Waiting on the Lord is coming to the realization that the strength of the natural man will not produce God's will. God has to teach you how to rely on His strength and power. Through waiting, God makes everything new about your life and gives you the power to walk in newness until death as clearly stated by the prophet: "But they that wait upon the LORD shall renew their strength; they shall mount up with wings as eagles; they shall run, and not be weary; and they shall walk, and not faint" (Isaiah 40:31).

Waiting is good, but waiting in some instances does not make you better for the other person. God is the one who gives the institution of marriage. All the talk about waiting for the right one will make no sense without God. Waiting on God is not waiting on material things like nice cars or houses. So waiting is never based on a time frame that one selects or sets.

Learn to flow with God and take action as necessary. Don't sit down and say you are waiting for an angel to take the next steps. If you sense in your spirit it is time to propose or break up a bad dating relationship, then go for it.

The purpose of waiting on the Lord is never to change a situation, people, or things. It is for His counsel, and once you sense His counsel within, it is time to act. There are no formulas to this. It flows spontaneously according to God's glory. Learn to hear from God through small things in line with His Word. God will never contradict His Word about life.

♥25♥
SIGNS TO HELP YOU DECIDE OR MAKE A CHOICE

I can't overemphasize the importance of self-denial, cross taking, and following Jesus. Self can blind us from seeing all potential problems and issues that lie ahead of us. Jesus knows your date or potential date better than you do. Jesus knows the deceiver, the liar, the useless, the idle, the abusive, the manipulator, the sex addict, the hidden secrets of every heart, and what the other person is trying to hide from you. Jesus wants us to follow Him so that He can show us what God wants for us.

In self, we have no idea what is truly good for us as self is only limited to external things. Self does not know or understand the spiritual status of people. The selfishness of self fails to see internal destructive persons. Self will not show you the other person because of its limitation.

The cross will teach us how to handle potential problems in a relationship. Why? Because Jesus has resolved all human issues in the flesh when He took the cross of the Father. If we stay at the path of the cross and take it continuously, Jesus will expose the devil that will try to show up in our lives. The Holy Spirit knows everything about everyone. He will show us signs about things not good for us as we stay in His presence.

God will not force His will on us, but He will show it to us, and it is up to us to accept or reject it. There are no steps, formulas, or programs to this. Let us learn the character of God, study His Word, and feed on Him so that we can know when He speaks to us in simple signs.

God does not go by an expert's advice to help you make an informed spiritual decision. God will deal with you on a personal level through simple things you can understand. Learn to listen to the still small voice of God. What may have worked for others, may not work for you because God is sovereign. He will work with you at your level of understanding if you follow the path of the cross.

The daily cross is never a man-made formula. God is sovereign and is not obligated to the formulas of men, but if we follow His lead, He can show us the signs to help us make serious decisions. When we take the cross and follow Jesus, we see things through the eyes of Jesus. Also, meditation and prayer and daily living the Word can help us notice behaviors or habits that may lead to deeper problems. Several small signs may lead to or indicate deeper problems underneath the surface. Through the Word, we may be able to look at situations, analyze them, and decide.

Looking at the attributes of God can help us in decision making. A.W Pink listed several attributes of God in his book the *Attributes of God*. But let us focus on a few here for the scope of this study:[xix]

- Sovereignty of God
- Holiness of God
- Patience of God
- Mercy of God
- Immutability of God
- Love of God
- Wrath of God
- Faithfulness of God
- Lovingkindness of God
- Foreknowledge of God

One important thing a Christian single needs to understand is that God is immutable. As stated by A.W Pink, "God has neither evolved, grown, nor improved. All that he is today, he has ever been, and ever will be."[xx]

In dating, take note of people who change all the time or whose ways are unstable. These are just simple things to take note of. If you are a true and dedicated Christian, do you really need someone who is deeply in love with the fashion and fads of the world? Every new thing that comes along they are with it. Their argument is built on the premise of "what is wrong with it? Everyone is doing it, so it must not be wrong." Certain things may not be necessarily wrong, but we must be willing to give up certain things for the sake of Christ and of the kingdom of God. "Love not the world, neither the things that are in the world. If any man love the world, the love of the Father is not in him" (1 John 2:15).

Particular things and habits are clearly worldly, and arguing about them in the dating period are signs of potential problems in a marriage. Some worldly movies, entertainment, and expert advice are extremely sinful, and most Christians still watch movies that excite their lustful passions and wild imaginations. They are unsettled and unsatisfied in the Lord. They are professing Christians but not practicing Christians.

Worldly ways and unstable Christianity in dating carried in marriage can lead to the breakup of a marriage. Variance in lifestyle is an issue you don't want to ignore. Marrying a professing Christian who is not dedicated to Christ, will not be dedicated in marriage. The relationship between Christ and the church is a picture of a lovely marriage. It is your choice to ignore clear signs because you love the person in self. Yes, Christian relationships can be miserable and fail when the cross is dropped.

Love is an attribute of God. The Bible clearly states God is love (1 John 1:5). The love of God is pure and perfect. It could not be patterned after defiled human emotions. Christians would only understand the love of God for them by allowing God's love to fill their hearts. God's love flows like water. It does not seek its own interest. God demonstrated this love sacrificially.

The entire life of Jesus on earth was full of spontaneous love. He recognizes needs and fulfills them. He did not sit down and wait for the problems of people to solve themselves. He responded to every problem with love. His love covered defects and deficiencies and people of every status.

I encourage you to study more about the love of God. God will show you signs about a person's love and the sacrifice they make to love others and the people of God. The love for the sake of Christ and of His kingdom is also a hint to look at. If you have to force someone to go to church or serve the Lord, you are heading for potential danger. People should love God without coercion. "God's love is not regulated by caprice, passion, or sentiment, but by principle. Just as his grace not at the expense of it, but through righteousness" (Romans 5:21).[xxi]

Forcing people to love you and love God is a clear indication they are not interested or serious about dating. If you marry them, you will be going to church and serving God by yourself. Dating at the cross should involve individuals already with a passion for seeking God at the cross. They should be actively involved in the body of Christ.

Divine love that went through death, burial, and resurrection is what keeps a marriage safe during all forms of storms. Even in difficult and challenging times, God's love for us never changes. Jesus Christ, the only begotten Son of the Father, was loved unconditionally from eternity to eternity. God's love for His Son Jesus did not diminish as Jesus faced humiliation, shame, and disgrace. He was always there and loved Him the same. How often trials and challenges affect couples today! Why, because human love changes based on circumstances. Is there a doubt of love in the relationship? Is the person in love with you when you take off the wig? Do they look at you strangely in times of physical or outward appearance changes? Are they busy comparing you to other men or women? Do they complement other men or women more than they do you? Do they have great admiration of celebrities of the opposite sex? These are things to think about. They portray an unstable frame of mind.

The love of God is found only in Jesus Christ. In other words, it is found only at the cross. At the cross, love is immutable. It is not attracted to any object or outside forces. The cross is the only channel through which love flows. The love of God does not flow through self. There are also several warning signs of self that God can show us clearly. Some signs are clear through observation and should not be ignored.

Let us assume you visit your date's family, and you observe adults on their phone, and no one goes to work. You also notice the environment is filthy and trashy. All they talk about is sports and entertainment. They exhibit an overwhelming abundance of idleness. Your date tells you that he or she has been job searching for years, but can't find one. They happen to be in a perpetual state of nothingness. They don't want to serve God either. Their drive for both spiritual things and family development is absent, but they keep telling you they love you. They talk more about how pretty or handsome you are, and that's it. They have nothing serious to talk about outside of what you look like and entertainment. The picture itself presents a clue for long term problems. All they talk about is being with you for life without knowing the cross required for a lifetime commitment. If these signs are not enough, what else would you need? Some folks know what they are running into from the beginning, but they ignore even simple and clear signs.

Spending more time on social media for fun and idleness is an indication of a problem person. Having an unhealthy curiosity can be addictive. Constant browsing habits of images and objects are influential in character building. Check their social media page, and if all they are talking about is nonsense and clicking like for everything, it is a problem. Check their timeline and friends. If they claim to love Jesus but are friends with porn stars, then they have a problem. Google and check their criminal records as well.

Satan can also use people in self to profess Christianity. They will come to church with you and read the Bible together with you. Sometimes they may not be agents of Satan but sincere Christians who are still in self. They may have professed Jesus, but have no intention of giving up self. Since self is the doorway to Satan, such believers are open to Satan and may be very dangerous—especially if they continue embracing self on a long term basis. This is why walking closely with Jesus is required for Jesus to show us what is hidden and needs to be exposed. Some things just can't be seen with the eyes of self.

People aren't going to be perfect, but some signs are definitely damaging to a long term relationship. Some signs are visible, while others are invisible. Clear visible signs should never be ignored. Never think they are not big deals; yes they are. Visible addictions such as idleness, laziness, pornography, lust, anger, aggression, selfishness, desperation, impatience, and disobedience should never be ignored.

Break up a dating relationship where people exhibit natural anger and control without any cause or don't obey basic things. Dating is not an anger management period. Christians in self who base dating just on self-attributes and ignore all other indicators of long term problems usually go through painful experiences they never wanted.

The culture and family influence of your date may affect both you and your children. Looking at the picture of friends, parents, and culture may give you an idea of what you want to live with. Bad cultural and family practices may create all sorts of issues. What a shock when addictive behaviors never seen in a dating period just pop up in an actual marriage. Depending on the person or situation, there would be some rude awakening. That's why destructive and chronic bad habits should never be overlooked.

Jesus should be allowed to lead. He will show us the addictive habits of self in a dating period. People who demonstrate habitual behaviors on which they have built their entire lives may not change overnight.

It is not your responsibility to deal with the chronic habits of others. Let them take it to the cross. I am not presenting perfection or self-righteousness here. The fact is there are certain troubling or abusive habits that will not lead to oneness. No one wants to live with abusive or destructive persons of self. Some people just think they can settle for any dysfunction and everything because they just want to be with someone so badly. Some will even quote Scriptures to stress their stubbornness and self-possessive ways. The oneness of God is not trashy and troubling.

On the whole, ask God to show you signs or patterns to give you peace about knowing whether someone is either for you or not for you. Consecrate yourself and ask God to show you what is good for you and He will do it. Desire God more than anything else, and everything will fall in place. God is sovereign, and He may show you signs exactly as He did for Abraham's servant. He has also given you His Word that is above every sign you may expect. Use the Word of God to understand and discover what He is doing. The ball is in your court. It is your responsibility to hear from God. I wish you the best always!

♥26♥
AVOIDING SURPRISES IN MARRIAGES

Surprise! Get ready for it. There are no marriages without surprises. The courtship period does not really give a full picture of what a person is in most cases. It is possible for people to suppress their feelings during the dating period. That is why the cross is very useful because it helps during both dating and marriage to reveal things and issues. People change, and when they change, their value changes. That is why the daily cross is very important in maintaining marriages. Most Christian couples with successful marriages have testified that changes did occur in their relationships but taking a cross that doesn't change helped them cope.

According to Scriptures, daily cross taking is required of all Christians. The daily cross is what God wants in the person of Christ manifested through the children of God. Christian dating is not an exemption to what God wants. Devotion to what God wants should be the daily lifestyle of a Christian.

Dedication to the ways of the cross in the dating period is not only required in dating but throughout the entire Christian life, which means marriage as well. It is loyalty to the cross that takes dating to marriage and throughout one's entire lifetime. Faithfulness to the cross will keep a marriage in focus when trials come. Satan will attack

Christian marriages viciously, but staying in the path of the cross will always lead to victory.

Every failed Christian marriage is a result of unfaithfulness not to people but the cross. We not only fail in relationships, but we also fail in so many areas when we stop being loyal to the cross. The purpose of self-denial and taking the daily cross is to sustain a commitment to a relationship with God. Daily means commitment.

When Jesus tells us to take the cross daily, it means a daily commitment to Him. The cross helps to deal with our daily flaws and faults. Everyone has weaknesses and flaws that will show up in marriage. The cross will strengthen us to bear the burden of one another's shortcomings.

Being one with Christ is the path to a beautiful gracious and spontaneous dating and loving relationship. A truthful and graceful life of dating can only be found in Jesus Christ (John 1:17). There is no grace and truth in human nature of self. Self is a liar and deceitful (John 8:44). Being loyal to the cross is what unites and establishes a Christian relationship. We can only be loyal, honest, and satisfied in a relationship if Christ is in us and running everything. Driving Christ out of our lives by choice exposes us to many failures and disappointments.

If we neglect the unpleasant process of conforming to the ways of the cross, we have no one to blame for the drama of self-love. As John Blanchard puts it: "that many people think of God as only a God of love, always on hand to help when things go wrong and bound in the end to forgive everybody's sins and receive them into heaven forever. This idea is fatally deceptive and misleading. The Bible certainly tells us that God is love (1 John 4:8), but also that He is majestic in holiness (Exodus 15:11), and that the wrath of God is revealed from heaven against all ungodliness and unrighteousness of men (Romans 1:18)."[xxii]

Christians need to realize God does not love and celebrate our sins and has no acceptance for sins. God's holiness requires the just punishment for sins. When Christ went to the cross, He substituted Himself to be punished for our sins, meaning God punishes every single sin. Just because someone else was punished for our sins, does not mean we should keep crucifying Christ daily with our sins.

We are justified by faith in Jesus Christ, and that is why we have the opportunity to confess our sins and be cleansed by the blood of Jesus when we sin (1 John 1:9). We should not continue to sin intentionally if we are in Christ. Let us ask God to help us in this area and not be deceived that God tolerates sin in dating. You will be a better lover by choosing and committing to the holy ways of the cross. Christians should not expect grace and truth of the cross in dating if they are not committed to the daily cross given by Christ.

Adapting an alternative dating lifestyle to the cross is embracing deception and the ways of self. An alternative lifestyle not only leads to more and more ungodliness; it is also walking another path God has not endorsed. In the end, that path leads to death. Unrighteousness feels good and correct to the disobedient: "There is a way which seemeth right unto a man, but the end thereof are the ways of death" (Proverbs 14:12).

How many times have we seen people who seem to be doing well, but all of a sudden destruction comes? God gives people chance after chance to repent and change their ways. Some have no intention of changing and have no remorse in their sins and will continue to live in deception by living the life they want. Choosing a life we want independent of the cross is disobedience to the cross. It drives us away from Christ and leads to death at the end.

Due to our natural life, we all have that selfish nature. Without the cross, we usually get something for ourselves. That's why the message of the cross is contrary to culture or human nature. The culture says it is all about you and how you feel as if love is a feeling.

Love is not a feeling, but the person of God in Christ. It is a commitment. It is looking at Jesus together. It is not focusing on self. Giving up of self is required for love to flow spontaneously out of the resurrected life. This is only accomplished by being committed to the cross continuously. Giving up the natural person of self is a lifetime commitment, not a once-in-awhile deal. It is a daily commitment to the cross.

The restless continuous desire and pursuit of the cross is the key to successful dating and marriage. Sustained commitment to the cross should always be the key to look for. Unstable commitment to the cross in dating would be a problem in marriage. Practicing commitment to the cross in the beginning may not be easy, but it is worthwhile. Commitment to the cross should be purposefully practiced until your life of the daily cross becomes natural to the point of it being fun.

There are no surprises in the life of the cross. God does not surprise those He loves with evil, and those in the path of the cross do not surprise each other with evil. The God of the Bible is a good God and will not tell us to serve Him just to surprise us with an evil end. Satan is good at introducing us to what we want by providing an illusion of a fake perfect life in the beginning only to lead us to destruction at the end.

The cross does not promote a perfect beginning of self to deceive us. The cross tells us to give up self on our way to joy and fulfillment. The cross may not start with worldly excitement but may lead to most fulfillment.

♥27♥
LESSONS LEARNED FROM SAMSON

The story of Sampson should be a warning to every single Christian that "you can date who you want and accept the consequences." Sampson was a very good example of dating who you want to date regardless of what the Word indicates.

Satan used women he prepared to feed on Sampson. As always, the purpose of Satan is to feed on flesh; He makes flesh appealing and desirable so that he can feed on people. Satan wanted to feed on Sampson, so he presented what was desirable to him. If you desire sinful fun and ways, Satan will be right there to feed on you until you are destroyed. What people wanted for themselves has destroyed them in many cases.

The story of Sampson is very relevant to what many singles within the church go through today. Some will never consider godly persons raised within the church. They will plainly say as Sampson did "I don't like them." Sampson was a very rebellious child compared to Isaac who was a child of the cross. The life of Samson in Judges chapters 14–16 is a timeless experience regarding dating outside the cross and self-love.

Although the experience may not be the same, Christians out of the path of the cross may experience the same headache like Sampson.

The timeless truth of not following the ways of God and the consequences are pretty much the same. Let us not focus on Judges 14:4, which portrays the sovereignty of God in human lives. Let us look at what we can learn from Samson's desire to date out of the cross as we can learn much from dating unbelievers or sinners.

Samson left the church to go after worldly women who tricked him many times. The self demon of lust completely blacked out the soul of Samson and allowed him to fall for the same scammer girls over and over and made the same mistakes over and over. He was tricked repeatedly with the same or similar game plan. Satan knew the self demon of Sampson and how to get to him.

Samson went where ungodly and seductive girls hung out and immediately got attracted to them. He just saw a pretty girl and immediately wanted to marry her based on the desires of his flesh. He approached his parents about his ungodly desire, but his parents warned him against dating or marrying an ungodly woman from an ungodly culture. Sampson would not listen. His reply was women in self will please him more. Women in self were able to entice him with feeding him their flesh.

The ungodly woman was already in self and dating for self was associated with others in self within her ungodly family, culture, and society. So, Sampson had to deal with numerous influences of people in his relationship. How many times have we seen the destruction of sexual lust within the church? People within the church today are told to do what they like as long as they are happy, but the end against God's Word is destruction.

Sexual lust is a very strong demon. It got hold of Sampson and never left him until he was destroyed as always the case; the end of self-life is total destruction. Sexual lust destroyed Sampson's calling and his relationship with God. Sampson was deceived to the point of believing his woman problem was more important than what God wanted.

From Scripture, the Spirit of God would usually move Sampson to do great things. This is an indication we can be filled with the Holy Spirit and still rebel, drop the cross, and return to self-life. In reality, many professing Christians usually would drop the cross and accept self to go after those they are attracted to regardless of how ungodly they may be.

Sampson had experienced the move of God and saw a worldly woman he wanted. He had no idea of the woman's background and family values. He just wanted her. He wanted to feed on her body. Although the woman was a Philistine, a people of the flesh and self, he just wanted her. It was love at first sight. This is the same thing that most singles born in the church go through as they lay down the cross and return to self. They even go out of their way to accept the consequences that may come with their choices.

One thing we should learn from Samson is to repent quickly and change our ways when we find ourselves drifting away from the truth. Sampson is exactly contrary to what the cross talks about. He had an issue of being patient and waiting on God. He could have chosen to find a woman among the people of God. Although the princesses of

God were more beautiful in every way, he was deceived to settle for less. Let us read a few verses of the situation and learn from it:

And Samson went down to Timnath, and saw a woman in Timnath of the daughters of the Philistines. And he came up, and told his father and his mother, and said, "I have seen a woman in Timnath of the daughters of the Philistines: now therefore get her for me to wife." Then his father and his mother said unto him, "Is there never a woman among the daughters of thy brethren, or among all my people, that thou goest to take a wife of the uncircumcised Philistines?" And Samson said unto his father, "Get her for me; for she pleaseth me well." Judges 14:1–3

And it came to pass on the seventh day, that they said unto Samson's wife, "Entice thy husband, that he may declare unto us the riddle, lest we burn thee and thy father's house with fire: have ye called us to take that we have? is it not so?" And Samson's wife wept before him, and said, "Thou dost but hate me, and lovest me not: thou hast put forth a riddle unto the children of my people, and hast not told it me." And he said unto her, "Behold, I have not told it my father nor my mother, and shall I tell it thee?" And she wept before him the seven days, while their feast lasted: and it came to pass on the seventh day, that he told her, because she lay sore upon him:

and she told the riddle to the children of her people. Judges 14:15–17

But it came to pass within a while after, in the time of wheat harvest that Samson visited his wife with a kid; and he said, "I will go in to my wife into the chamber." But her father would not suffer him to go in. And her father said, "I verily thought that thou hadst utterly hated her; therefore I gave her to thy companion: is not her younger sister fairer than she? take her, I pray thee, instead of her." And Samson said concerning them, "Now shall I be more blameless than the Philistines, though I do them a displeasure." And Samson went and caught three hundred foxes, and took firebrands, and turned tail to tail, and put a firebrand in the midst between two tails. And when he had set the brands on fire, he let them go into the standing corn of the Philistines, and burnt up both the shocks, and also the standing corn, with the vineyards and olives. Then the Philistines said, "Who hath done this?" And they answered, "Samson, the son-in-law of the Timnite, because he had taken his wife, and given her to his companion." And the Philistines came up, and burnt her and her father with fire. And Samson said unto them, "Though ye have done this, yet will I be avenged of you, and after that I will cease." And he smote them hip and thigh with a great slaughter: and he went down and dwelt in the top of the rock Etam. Judges 15:1–8.

Then went Samson to Gaza, and saw there an harlot, and went in unto her... And it came to pass afterward, that he loved a woman in the valley of Sorek, whose name was Delilah. And the lords of the Philistines came up unto her, and said unto her, "Entice him, and see wherein his great strength lieth, and by what means we may prevail against him, that we may bind him to afflict him; and we will give thee every one of us eleven hundred pieces of silver." And Delilah said to Samson, "Tell me, I pray thee, wherein thy great strength lieth, and wherewith thou mightest be bound to afflict thee." Judges 16:1–6

And she said unto him, "How canst thou say, I love thee, when thine heart is not with me? thou hast mocked me these three times, and hast not told me wherein thy great strength lieth." And it came to pass, when she pressed him daily with her words, and urged him, so that his soul was vexed unto death; That he told her all his heart, and said unto her, "There hath not come a razor upon mine head; for I have been a Nazarite unto God from my mother's womb: if I be shaven, then my strength will go from me, and I shall become weak, and be like any other man." And when Delilah saw that he had told her all his heart, she sent and called for the lords of the Philistines, saying, "Come up this once, for he hath shewed me all his heart." Then the lords of the Philistines came up unto her, and brought money in their hand. And she made him sleep upon her knees; and she called for a man, and she caused him to shave off the seven locks of his head;

and she began to afflict him, and his strength went from him. And she said, "The Philistines be upon thee, Samson." And he awoke out of his sleep, and said, "I will go out as at other times before, and shake myself." And he wist not that the LORD was departed from him. Judges 16:15–20

From Samson's bad experience as a result of self, we can learn many lessons. One does not have to go through the same experience but can gain from it through learning. The love of self placed Sampson in a position of trusting women more than God. Because the devil noticed his self desire, he took advantage of it. Sexual lust is a very strong demon. It got a hold of Sampson and never left Sampson until he was destroyed. As always the case, the end self-life is total destruction.

Sampson ignored clear warnings of the word from his parent for the popular culture of the day. Arguing and resisting godly parental advice and biblical counseling is why many young people encounter long term or permanent relationship issues.

As Sampson became engrossed in the world's culture, he became spiritually dead. He was slow to learn and repent quickly. This is very similar to many within the church today. They were born in the church and grew up within godly families, but they allowed Satan to enter them by elevating sin above reality. As they fall for lies, Satan gets his way by giving them much trouble and pain, Disobedience to God and His cross in a relationship leads to never-ending drama.

♥28♥
LESSONS LEARNED FROM ISAAC

Isaac was not pressed or in a rush to look for a date. He was in a godly environment. He loved and enjoyed his status of singleness. He was committed to the place and status of God's will. Isaac was raised in an environment and culture of godly influences. These sincere, godly influences played a big role in his relationship. The goal of godly influences in Isaac's relationship was the cross, meaning what God wants.

In the world, the role of godly influences may be downplayed as arranged marriages. Arranged marriages are marriages organized by pagan religions for the benefit of self. But introducing a godly person from a godly family to another godly person in a godly family is not an arranged marriage. An introduction is not coercing or forcing. It is okay if things work and okay if they don't work.

Advising a young person not to date an unbeliever is also not coercing or forcing. It is their choice, but those of us who have children at dating age must tell them what the Bible says about the issue, and it is their choice to obey or disobey. God takes faith in the family very important.

The life of Isaac was very admirable as God picked Rebekah for him. He was in his forties and not looking for anyone, nor was he desperate. He understood the act of God. He learned from his dad, Abraham, that God can lead him to the best. All he had to do was to accept the cross when given. He saw the demonstration of God in his father. He learned from his father how to trust God. Today, we can learn much from older saints and godly people. We can gain from their experience if we are humble and willing to learn.

From Isaac, we should learn that dating at the cross has nothing to do with body shapes, figures, or appearance. The Word says that Rebekah was very beautiful. Isaac did not pick Rebekah, but Rebekah was God's choice for him. Isaac never saw Rebekah before he made a decision; he did not know how beautiful Rebekah was. He did not run through a series of women before he settled with Rebekah. He was set up with Rebekah through prayer. And when God answered Abraham's prayer, Isaac accepted Rebekah. This clearly portrays that Christian love is a commitment to God's will. It is not what we always want for ourselves.

Rebekah was an answer to prayer. And the prayer was answered quickly because God knew it was Isaac's time to have a wife. She was a validation of a divine sign. She was willing to come out of self to serve a need. She served freely without arguments, requests, or reservation. She showed kindness to people she didn't know. She was the full package of beauty, service, and loyalty. She went on to be a mother who understood the daily cross and the promise of God. She recognized the separation between her two kids as flesh and spirit.

Even with her kids, she favored the more spiritual child over the more fleshy child.

Although Rebekah and Isaac were nowhere near perfect, their match was made from heaven. I have no idea whether they understood the daily cross or the will of God at the time due to the favoritism they showed among their sons. But let us focus on how they met and the lessons to be learned.

The entire set up of Isaac's relationship was based on the cross. Rebekah was never forced or coerced. No money was offered to Rebecca's parents upfront prior to meeting Rebekah. Rebekah was a result of a prayer request.

One thing we should learn is that marriage is a commitment to the cross. Read the Scripture and learn some lessons from Isaac and Rebekah:

And Abraham was old, and well stricken in age: and the LORD had blessed Abraham in all things. And Abraham said unto his eldest servant of his house, that ruled over all that he had, "Put, I pray thee, thy hand under my thigh: And I will make thee swear by the LORD, the God of heaven, and the God of the earth, that thou shalt not take a wife unto my son of the daughters of the Canaanites, among whom I dwell: But thou shalt go unto my country, and to my kindred, and take a wife unto my son Isaac." And the servant said unto him, "Peradventure the woman will not be willing to follow me unto this land: must I needs bring thy son again unto the land from whence thou camest?" And Abraham said unto him, "Beware thou that thou bring not my son thither again. The LORD God of heaven, which took me from my father's house, and from the land of my kindred, and which spake unto me, and that sware unto me, saying, 'Unto thy seed will I give this land; he shall send his angel before thee, and thou shalt take a wife unto my son from thence.' And if the woman will not be willing to follow thee, then thou shalt be clear from this my oath: only bring not my son thither again." And the servant put his hand under the thigh of Abraham his master, and sware to him concerning that matter. And the servant took ten camels of the camels of his master, and departed; for all the goods of his master were in his hand: and he arose, and went to Mesopotamia, unto the city of Nahor. And he made his camels to kneel down without the city by a well of water at the time of the evening, even the time that women go out to draw water. And he said "O LORD God of my master Abraham, I pray thee, send me good speed this day, and shew kindness unto my master Abraham. Behold, I stand here by the well of water; and the daughters of the men of the city come out to draw water: And let it come to pass, that the damsel to whom I shall say, 'Let down thy pitcher, I pray thee, that I may drink;' and she shall say, 'Drink, and I will give thy camels drink also:' let the same be she that thou hast appointed for thy servant Isaac; and thereby shall I know that thou hast shewed kindness unto my master." And it came to pass, before he had done speaking, that, behold, Rebekah came out, who was born to Bethuel, son of Milcah, the wife of

Nahor, Abraham's brother, with her pitcher upon her shoulder. And the

damsel was very fair to look upon, a virgin, neither had any man known her: and she went down to the well, and filled her pitcher, and came up. And the servant ran to meet her, and said, "Let me, I pray thee, drink a little water of thy pitcher." And she said, "Drink, my lord:" and she hasted, and let down her pitcher upon her hand, and gave him drink. And when she had done giving him drink, she said, "I will draw water for thy camels also, until they have done drinking." And she hasted, and emptied her pitcher into the trough, and ran again unto the well to draw water, and drew for all his camels. And the man wondering at her held his peace, to wit whether the LORD had made his journey prosperous or not. And it came to pass, as the camels had done drinking, that the man took a golden earring of half a shekel weight, and two bracelets for her hands of ten shekels weight of gold; And said, "Whose daughter art thou? tell me, I pray thee: is there room in thy father's house for us to lodge in?" And she said unto him, "I am the daughter of Bethuel the son of Milcah, which she bare unto Nahor." She said moreover unto him, "We have both straw and provender enough, and room to lodge in." And the man bowed down his head, and worshiped the LORD. And he said, "Blessed be the LORD God of my master Abraham, who hath not left destitute my master of his mercy and his truth: I being in the way, the LORD led me to the house of my master's brethren." And the

damsel ran, and told them of her mother's house these things.
Genesis 24:1–28

The manner in which Rebekah was found for Isaac was so unique. Abraham's servant prayed to God for a sign, and God answered. There was nothing desperate and crazy. Everything flowed spontaneously while Isaac was minding his business. Isaac had a sincere spiritual mentor in his father. One thing to learn from Isaac was he did not argue or resist experienced godly advice.

It is pitiful that very little is done within the church in developing young people today for relationships and life. We have become like the world by telling them to do what they like and what feels good to them right within the church. The result is raising up a generation that has no interest in doing what God wants but at the same time want to be Christians as a status. The cross never fails, and if we follow the ways of the cross, we will have a beautiful life.

♥ENDNOTES♥

[i] Fenelon, *The Seeking Heart*. Christian Books Publishing House, c1992 p. 12

[ii] Fenelon, *The Seeking Heart*. Christian Books Publishing House, c1992 p. 171

[iii] Simpson, A.B. *The Self Life and the Christ Life*. First Rate Publishers, chapter one

[iv] Bernard of Clairvaux. *The Love of God and Spiritual Friendship*. Edited by James Houston, General Editor of Classics of Faith and Devotion. Multnomah Press, c1983

[v] Simpson, A.B. *The Self Life and the Christ Life*. First Rate Publishers, chapter one

[vi] Pink, A. W. *The Attributes of God*, Chapel Library c1930 p. 68

[vii] Genda, John. *The Mandatory Cross Life*. GPS c2018

[viii] Simpson, A.B. *The Self Life and the Christ Life*. First Rate Publishers. Chapter one

[ix] Bernard of Clairvaux. *The Love of God and Spiritual Friendship*. Edited by James Houston, General Editor of Classics of Faith and Devotion. Multnomah Press, c1983 1090–1153

[x] Krznaric, Roman. "The Ancient Greeks' 6 Words for Love (And Why Knowing Them Can Change Your Life)." Yes Magazine. https://www.yesmagazine.org/happiness/the-ancient-greeks-6-words-for-love-and-why-knowing-them-can-change-your-life

[xi] Simpson, A.B. *The Cross Life and the Christ Life*. First Rate Publishers. Chapter one

[xii] Krznaric, Roman. "The Ancient Greeks' 6 Words for Love (And Why Knowing Them Can Change Your Life)." Yes Magazine. https://www.yesmagazine.org/happiness/the-ancient-greeks-6-words-for-love-and-why-knowing-them-can-change-your-life

[xiii] Bernard of Clairvaux. *The Love of God and Spiritual Friendship*. Edited by James Houston, General Editor of Classics of Faith and Devotion. Multnomah Press, c1983

[xiv] Ibid.

[xv] Fenelon, *The Seeking Heart.* Christian Books Publishing House, c1992 p. 171

[xvi] "G3877 – parakoloutheó." From the *NAS Exhaustive Concordance of the Bible with Hebrew-Aramaic and Greek Dictionaries* Copyright © 1981, 1998 by The Lockman Foundation. https://biblehub.com/greek/3877.htm

[xvii] Ibid.

[xviii] Lawrence, Brother. *The Practice of the Presence of God.* Whitaker House. c1982

[xix] Pink, A.W. *Attributes of God.* Chapel Library, c1930

[xx] Ibid.

[xxi] Ibid.

[xxii] Blanchard, John. *Why the Cross?* EP Books, c2011. p 35–36

♥About the Author♥

It is not about the author, but about the cross of Jesus Christ. Therefore, this excerpt is only for informational purposes for the curious.

The author desires readers to view him as one who was once bound and controlled by the prince and power of the air and walked according to the course of this world, the spirit that now worketh in the children of disobedience (Ephesians 2:2). He was unfit and unworthy to take the cross and undeserving of grace, but the grace of God which carries salvation to all still appeared to him through a God who so dearly loves him and gave His only Son for him (John 3:16). His unworthiness of the grace which has been so freely poured on him makes him see himself as the least among the saints to whom this grace was given to preach the unsearchable riches of Christ (Ephesians 3:8). His greatest accomplishment is accepting this unmerited grace through repentance.

The author lives in western Maryland with his family and is a citizen of God's kingdom whose current spiritual address within the body of Christ is Clean Page International Fellowship.

Although the author is ordained and holds degrees in Cybersecurity, Biblical Studies, Paralegal Studies, and multiple certifications, he has no glory in such accomplishments. He counts all things as dung for the sake of the humble cross of Christ, not to be boastful of any status (Philippians 3:8).

The author prays not to be in the sad, empty state of placing much emphasis on things of vanity as human status and accomplishments as stated by the preacher "Vanity of vanities, saith the Preacher, vanity of vanities; all is vanity" (Ecclesiastes 1:2). He is humbled to pursue the cross continually.

John Genda is also the organizer of Clean Page Fellowship, an association of individuals who believe in pursuing God and encouraging others to do likewise by reaching out. Initiated by the Holy Spirit, John Genda recently started the BEAM (Backyard Missions and Evangelism) encouraging local churches to do all within their power to share the gospel beginning within the one-mile radius of their church and extending further. He places a high priority on prayer and evangelism. He also offers free cross-life leadership training for startup churches and young people. Please contact **www.johngenda.org** for further information.

www.ingramcontent.com/pod-product-compliance
Lightning Source LLC
LaVergne TN
LVHW051124080426
835510LV00018B/2226

9 780974 722412